CONTENTS

D1133910

p.87

The Fabulous '50s
5

Streamlining the '60s
21

p.25

Eclectic Tastes of the '70s
45

p.68

The Adventurous '80s
61

p.30

Cooking "American" in the '90s
83

p.96

p.78

Fifty favorites from 50 years

Since the first BAKE-OFF® Contest, nearly 4,000 finalists have vied for the top spot. Yet, as with any contest, there can be only a handful of money winners. While you may be familiar with many of the Grand Prize Winners, there are other wonderful recipes that didn't catch the judges' attention. We asked consumers and long-time BAKE-OFF® Contest employees to identify their favorites. Collectively, these 50 recipes epitomize the venerable Pillsbury BAKE-OFF® Contest and represent a piece of American cooking history.

Alice R. Reese receives a warm welcome home after winning Pillsbury's 13th BAKE-OFF® Contest for her recipe called Candy Bar Cookies.

Little did these food editors know in 1949 that this competition would become America's premier cooking and baking contest.

In the beginning

In 1949, the Pillsbury BAKE-OFF® Contest began as the "Grand National Recipe and Baking Contest" held at the elegant Waldorf-Astoria Hotel, New York City. Executives at Pillsbury's advertising agency created the contest as an opportunity for American homemakers to share their treasured recipes. And they wanted to celebrate the company's 80th birthday. Response to the contest was so great that Pillsbury decided to hold it again the following year, and the year after that, until it became an institution. Almost immediately, the media dubbed the Grand National the BAKE-OFF® Contest. The name fit so well that the company adopted it as the contest's official name.

The Pillsbury BAKE-OFF® Contest, now held every other year (and celebrating its 50th anniversary this year), remains the nation's most prestigious cooking and baking competition. The contest not only reflects food trends but also sets the trends in American cooking.

BAKE-OFF® bloopers

What's behind the scenes? A few "oops," "oh nos" and "watch outs!"

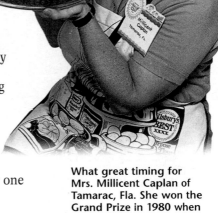

- To accommodate the Grand Ballroom's lack of alternating electrical current during the first contest held at New York City's Waldorf-Astoria Hotel, a power cable from the hotel had to be tapped into the New York Central Railroad for current to run the 100 contest ranges.

- In 1988, at the site of the 33rd contest in San Diego, CA, a large, plastic foam Doughboy was stolen from the hotel lobby by kids on a lark. Ransom calls followed until the Doughboy was returned, wearing sunglasses and riding in a convertible.

- A pie baker set her finished creation on the chair beside her range to cool before judging—then absentmindedly sat on it. (Since rules allow making the recipe three times, she baked another one for the judges!)

What great timing for Mrs. Millicent Caplan of Tamarac, Fla. She won the Grand Prize in 1980 when the top award was bumped from $25,000 to $40,000.

A million-dollar millennium

You could be the first BAKE-OFF® Contest million-dollar winner in the new millennium! For details on entering the 39th Pillsbury BAKE-OFF® Contest, to be held in San Francisco in February 2000, visit the web site at **www.bakeoff.com.**

From ballroom to kitchen

Compare a photo of the BAKE-OFF® competition in progress today with that of the first contest, and you'll find that little has changed to transform the hotel ballroom into 100 mini-kitchens.

"It's a phenomenal thing to see," observed one individual involved with the contest set-up. "There's an army of people. And everything is synchronized. As soon as one range goes into position, a cabinet is immediately set next to it, then the next and the next. The precision of the entire process is amazing."

Setting up the competition floor with its 100 mini-kitchens requires lots of people power — about 200 workers logging more than 10,000 hours.

The Fabulous '50s

The economic boom of the postwar years led to a belief that America had abundance in all things. The good life was evident in rich, filling meals and glamorous desserts. Since women rarely worked outside the home, housewives spent hours in the kitchen.

Television, a new invention, emphasized American women in the role of mother. In programs like "Father Knows Best," Mom most often appeared in an apron, with a rolling pin.

The single required ingredient in recipes of the earliest contests was Pillsbury BEST® Flour. Scratch cakes represented the largest category of BAKE-OFF® entries in the 1950s, followed by yeast and quick breads, pies and cookies, with few main dishes in the finals.

1. Food experts taste-test the recipes of 25 teens competing in the junior contest.

2. Although convenience foods began to appear during the 1950s, many believed that long lists of ingredients, complex preparation and elaborate presentation symbolized good cooking.

3. Mona Benn, Linden, Pa., perfected a "hand-me-down" recipe from her great-grandmother to earn a trip to the 1950 junior competition.

4. It's no wonder Opal Couch, Orchard, Neb., looked so serious. She was preparing her recipe in front of The Duke and Duchess of Windsor, guests of honor at the Second Grand National Recipe and Baking Contest.

French Silk Chocolate Pie

Pictured on right

Prep Time: 50 minutes (Ready in 2 hours 50 minutes)

Mrs. Kendall E. Cooper of Silver Spring, Maryland, brought this ultra-rich chocolate pie to the 3rd BAKE-OFF® Contest. Her original recipe included raw eggs, but this updated, safer version calls for pasteurized eggs or egg product.

Ingredient Info

Pasteurized eggs have been heated to a temperature that destroys disease-producing bacteria but does not cook the eggs. These eggs are safe to eat without additional cooking. Look for pasteurized eggs in the dairy case. Each egg inside the carton is clearly marked pasteurized. Because the eggs in this recipe are not cooked, pasteurized eggs or fat-free egg product must be used.

Kitchen Tip

For directions on making chocolate curls, see the Kitchen Tip on p. 68.

CRUST
1 Pillsbury Refrigerated Pie Crust (from 15-oz. pkg.)

FILLING
3 oz. unsweetened chocolate, cut into pieces
1 cup butter, softened (do not use margarine)
1 cup sugar
½ teaspoon vanilla
4 *pasteurized eggs* or 1 cup refrigerated or frozen fat-free egg product, thawed

TOPPING
½ cup sweetened whipped cream
Chocolate curls, if desired

1 Heat oven to 450°F. Prepare pie crust as directed on package for *one-crust baked shell* using 9-inch pie pan. Bake at 450°F. for 9 to 11 minutes or until light golden brown. Cool 30 minutes or until completely cooled.

2 Melt chocolate in small saucepan over low heat; cool. In small bowl, beat butter until fluffy. Gradually add sugar, beating until light and fluffy. Add cooled chocolate and vanilla; blend well.

3 Add eggs 1 at a time, beating at high speed for 2 minutes after each addition. Beat until mixture is smooth and fluffy. Pour into cooled baked shell. Refrigerate at least 2 hours before serving. Top with whipped cream and chocolate curls. Store in refrigerator.

10 servings

NUTRITION INFORMATION PER SERVING:
SERVING SIZE: 1/10 of Recipe

Calories		470	Calories from Fat	320
			% DAILY VALUE	
Total Fat	35 g		54%	
Saturated	20 g		100%	
Cholesterol	155 mg		52%	
Sodium	300 mg		13%	
Total Carbohydrate	34 g		11%	
Dietary Fiber	1 g		4%	
Sugars	22 g			
Protein	4 g			
Vitamin A	20%		Vitamin C	0%
Calcium	4%		Iron	6%

DIETARY EXCHANGES: 1 Starch, 1-1/2 Fruit, 7 Fat
OR 2-1/2 Carbohydrate, 7 Fat

Peanut Blossoms

Pictured on left

Prep Time: 1 hour

1¾ cups Pillsbury BEST® All Purpose Flour
½ cup sugar
½ cup firmly packed brown sugar
1 teaspoon baking soda
½ teaspoon salt
½ cup shortening
½ cup peanut butter
2 tablespoons milk
1 teaspoon vanilla
1 egg
Sugar
48 milk chocolate candy kisses, unwrapped

1 Heat oven to 375°F. Lightly spoon flour into measuring cup; level off. In large bowl, combine flour, ½ cup sugar, brown sugar, baking soda, salt, shortening, peanut butter, milk, vanilla and egg; mix at low speed until stiff dough forms. Shape dough into 1-inch balls; roll in sugar. Place 2 inches apart on ungreased cookie sheets.

2 Bake at 375°F. for 10 to 12 minutes or until golden brown. Immediately top each cookie with 1 candy kiss, pressing down firmly so cookie cracks around edge; remove from cookie sheets.

4 dozen cookies

HIGH ALTITUDE (ABOVE 3500 FEET): No change.

NUTRITION INFORMATION PER SERVING:
SERVING SIZE: 1 Cookie

Calories	100	Calories from Fat	45
		% DAILY VALUE	
Total Fat	5 g	8%	
Saturated	2 g	10%	
Cholesterol	5 mg	2%	
Sodium	65 mg	3%	
Total Carbohydrate	12 g	4%	
Dietary Fiber	0 g	0%	
Sugars	8 g		
Protein	2 g		
Vitamin A	0%	Vitamin C	0%
Calcium	0%	Iron	2%

DIETARY EXCHANGES: 1 Fruit, 1 Fat **OR** 1 Carbohydrate, 1 Fat

Recipe Fact
Freda Smith of Gibsonburg, Ohio, created this chocolate-topped peanut butter cookie for her grandsons. Her recipe has been a popular treat in households across America since she brought it to the 9th BAKE-OFF® Contest in 1957.

Kitchen Tip
To save time, unwrap the candy kisses while the first sheet of cookies is baking.

Storage Tip
The chocolate kisses on these cookies stay soft even after the cookie base has cooled. To help the chocolates set more quickly, place the cooled cookies in the refrigerator for a few minutes. Make sure the chocolates are completely set before storing the cookies in an airtight container.

From top:
Cherry Winks p. 10,
Peanut Blossoms

Recipe Fact

This popular cookie was entered in the BAKE-OFF® Contest in 1950 by Ruth Derousseau. She entered her recipe in the junior division and won $5,000.

Kitchen Tips

Chop the maraschino cherries then drain them on paper towels to eliminate excess moisture.

To crush the corn flakes without mess, enclose them in a resealable plastic food storage bag and crush them with a rolling pin or heavy pan.

To coat the cookies with cereal, just drop the dough into the mixture in the plastic bag.

Cherry Winks

Pictured on page 8

Prep Time: 1 hour 20 minutes

1 cup sugar
¾ cup shortening
2 tablespoons milk
1 teaspoon vanilla
2 eggs
2¼ cups Pillsbury BEST® All Purpose Flour
1 teaspoon baking powder
½ teaspoon baking soda
½ teaspoon salt
1 cup chopped pecans
1 cup chopped dates
⅓ cup chopped maraschino cherries, well drained
1½ cups coarsely crushed corn flakes cereal
15 maraschino cherries, quartered

1 In large bowl, combine sugar and shortening; beat well. Add milk, vanilla and eggs; mix well. Lightly spoon flour into measuring cup; level off. Add flour, baking powder, baking soda and salt; mix well. Stir in pecans, dates and ⅓ cup chopped cherries. If necessary, cover with plastic wrap; refrigerate 15 minutes for easier handling.

2 Heat oven to 375°F. Grease cookie sheets. Drop dough by rounded teaspoonfuls into cereal; thoroughly coat. Shape into balls. Place 2 inches apart on greased cookie sheets. Lightly press maraschino cherry quarter into top of each ball.

3 Bake at 375°F. for 10 to 15 minutes or until light golden brown. Remove from cookie sheets.

5 dozen cookies

HIGH ALTITUDE (ABOVE 3500 FEET): No change.

NUTRITION INFORMATION PER SERVING:
SERVING SIZE: 1 Cookie

Calories	90		Calories from Fat	35
			% DAILY VALUE	
Total Fat	4	g	6%	
Saturated	1	g	5%	
Cholesterol	5	mg	2%	
Sodium	70	mg	3%	
Total Carbohydrate	12	g	4%	
Dietary Fiber	1	g	2%	
Sugars	6	g		
Protein	1	g		
Vitamin A	0%		Vitamin C	0%
Calcium	0%		Iron	6%

DIETARY EXCHANGES: 1/2 Starch, 1/2 Fruit, 1/2 Fat **OR** 1 Carbohydrate, 1/2 Fat

Split Seconds

Pictured on page 13

Prep Time: 1 hour 15 minutes

²/₃ cup sugar
³/₄ cup margarine or butter, softened
2 teaspoons vanilla
1 egg
2 cups Pillsbury BEST® All Purpose Flour
¹/₂ teaspoon baking powder
¹/₂ cup red jelly or preserves

1 Heat oven to 350°F. In large bowl, combine sugar and margarine; beat until light and fluffy. Add vanilla and egg; blend well. Lightly spoon flour into measuring cup; level off. Add flour and baking powder; mix well.

2 Divide dough into 4 equal parts. On lightly floured surface, shape each part into 12×³/₄-inch roll; place on ungreased cookie sheets. Using handle of wooden spoon or finger, make depression about ¹/₂ inch wide and ¹/₄ inch deep lengthwise down center of each roll. Fill each roll with 2 tablespoons jelly.

3 Bake at 350°F. for 15 to 20 minutes or until light golden brown. Cool slightly. Cut each baked roll diagonally into 12 cookies. Remove from cookie sheets; cool on wire racks.

4 dozen cookies

HIGH ALTITUDE (ABOVE 3500 FEET): No change.

NUTRITION INFORMATION PER SERVING:
SERVING SIZE: 1 Cookie

Calories	70	Calories from Fat	25
		% DAILY VALUE	
Total Fat	3 g	5%	
Saturated	1 g	5%	
Cholesterol	4 mg	1%	
Sodium	40 mg	2%	
Total Carbohydrate	9 g	3%	
Dietary Fiber	0 g	0%	
Sugars	4 g		
Protein	1 g		
Vitamin A	2%	Vitamin C	0%
Calcium	0%	Iron	0%

DIETARY EXCHANGES: 1/2 Starch, 1/2 Fat
OR 1/2 Carbohydrate, 1/2 Fat

COOK'S NOTES

Recipe Fact
Karin Fellows of Silver Spring, Maryland, learned to cook in Sweden. She entered this family-favorite shortbread cookie in the 6th BAKE-OFF® Contest. Her recipe is one of our classics.

Ingredient Substitution
Try filling these delicious cookies with your favorite homemade or specialty jam, jelly or preserves.

Make It Special
Dust the cookies with powdered sugar or drizzle them with powdered sugar icing.

Nutmeg Cookie Logs

Pictured on right

Prep Time: 1 hour 20 minutes

Recipe Fact
Julia Woods of South Charleston, West Virginia, created this spicy-sweet cookie for the 1956 contest. Her recipe has become a favorite among our home economists, especially during the holidays.

Ingredient Info
Nutmeg comes from the seed of a tropical evergreen tree native to the Spice Islands. (The seed is covered in a lacy coating that is dried and ground into the spice called mace.) Nutmeg can be purchased whole or ground. Store nutmeg in a jar in a cool, dark place.

Kitchen Tip
For the freshest nutmeg flavor, purchase whole seeds and grate the spice just before use. Small nutmeg graters can be purchased at kitchenware stores.

COOKIES
¾ cup sugar
1 cup margarine or butter, softened
2 teaspoons vanilla
2 teaspoons rum extract
1 egg
3 cups Pillsbury BEST® All Purpose Flour
1 teaspoon nutmeg

FROSTING
2 cups powdered sugar
3 tablespoons margarine or butter, softened
¾ teaspoon rum extract
¼ teaspoon vanilla
2 to 3 tablespoons half-and-half or milk
Nutmeg

1 In large bowl, combine sugar, 1 cup margarine, 2 teaspoons vanilla, 2 teaspoons rum extract and egg; beat until light and fluffy. Lightly spoon flour into measuring cup; level off. Stir in flour and 1 teaspoon nutmeg; mix well. If necessary, cover with plastic wrap; refrigerate 30 to 45 minutes for easier handling.

2 Heat oven to 350°F. Divide dough into 12 pieces. On lightly floured surface, shape each piece of dough into long rope, ½ inch in diameter (about 15 inches long). Cut into 3-inch lengths; place on ungreased cookie sheets.

3 Bake at 350°F. for 12 to 15 minutes or until bottoms are light golden brown. Immediately remove from cookie sheets. Cool 15 minutes or until completely cooled.

4 In small bowl, combine all frosting ingredients except nutmeg, adding enough half-and-half for desired spreading consistency. Spread on top and sides of cookies. If desired, mark frosting with tines of fork to resemble bark. Sprinkle lightly with nutmeg. Let stand until frosting is set. Store in tightly covered container.

5 dozen cookies

HIGH ALTITUDE (ABOVE 3500 FEET): No change.

NUTRITION INFORMATION PER SERVING:
SERVING SIZE: 1 Cookie

Calories	80	Calories from Fat	35
		% DAILY VALUE	
Total Fat	4 g		6%
Saturated	1 g		5%
Cholesterol	4 mg		1%
Sodium	45 mg		2%
Total Carbohydrate	11 g		4%
Dietary Fiber	0 g		0%
Sugars	6 g		
Protein	1 g		
Vitamin A	4%	Vitamin C	0%
Calcium	0%	Iron	0%

DIETARY EXCHANGES: 1/2 Starch, 1 Fat
OR 1/2 Carbohydrate, 1 Fat

Clockwise from top:
Caramel Cream Sandwich
Cookies p. 14, Nutmeg Cookie
Logs, Split Seconds p. 11

The Fabulous '50s   13

Recipe Fact

Helen Beckman was only 15 years old when she entered the 6th BAKE-OFF® Contest. She took home $2,000 for this sandwich cookie, which has become a Pillsbury favorite.

Kitchen Tip

If the frosting becomes stiff before all the cookies are filled, thin it with additional milk.

Storage Tip

Store the leftover egg white in a tightly covered container in the refrigerator and use within 2 days. Add it to scrambled eggs or an omelet.

Caramel Cream Sandwich Cookies

Pictured on page 13

Prep Time: 1 hour 15 minutes

COOKIES
¾ cup firmly packed brown sugar
1 cup butter or margarine, softened
1 egg yolk
2 cups Pillsbury BEST® All Purpose Flour
FROSTING
2 tablespoons butter (do not use margarine)
1¼ cups powdered sugar
½ teaspoon vanilla
4 to 5 teaspoons milk

1 In large bowl, combine brown sugar and 1 cup butter; beat until light and fluffy. Add egg yolk; blend well. Lightly spoon flour into measuring cup; level off. Add flour; mix well. If necessary, cover with plastic wrap; refrigerate 15 minutes for easier handling.

2 Heat oven to 325°F. Shape dough into 1-inch balls. Place 2 inches apart on ungreased cookie sheets. With fork dipped in flour, flatten each to 1½-inch round.

3 Bake at 325°F. for 10 to 14 minutes or until light golden brown. Cool 1 minute; remove from cookie sheets. Cool 15 minutes or until completely cooled.

4 Meanwhile, in medium saucepan, heat 2 tablespoons butter over medium heat until light golden brown, stirring constantly. Remove from heat. Stir in all remaining frosting ingredients, adding enough milk for desired spreading consistency; blend until smooth. Spread scant 1 teaspoon frosting between 2 cooled cookies. Repeat with remaining frosting and cookies.

30 sandwich cookies

HIGH ALTITUDE (ABOVE 3500 FEET): No change.

NUTRITION INFORMATION PER SERVING:
SERVING SIZE: 1 Sandwich Cookie

Calories	140	Calories from Fat	60
		% DAILY VALUE	
Total Fat	7 g	11%	
Saturated	4 g	20%	
Cholesterol	25 mg	8%	
Sodium	75 mg	3%	
Total Carbohydrate	17 g	6%	
Dietary Fiber	0 g	0%	
Sugars	10 g		
Protein	1 g		
Vitamin A	6%	Vitamin C	0%
Calcium	0%	Iron	2%

DIETARY EXCHANGES: 1/2 Starch, 1/2 Fruit, 1-1/2 Fat
OR 1 Carbohydrate, 1-1/2 Fat

Sweet Petals

Pictured on page 17

Prep Time: 40 minutes (Ready in 2 hours 40 minutes)

COFFEE CAKE
2½ to 3 cups Pillsbury BEST® All Purpose Flour
  2 tablespoons sugar
  1 teaspoon salt
  1 pkg. active dry yeast
  ¾ cup milk
  ¼ cup water
  3 tablespoons shortening
FILLING
  ½ cup finely chopped nuts
  ½ cup sugar
  2 tablespoons brown sugar
  1 teaspoon cinnamon
  ½ cup butter, melted
GLAZE
  ½ cup powdered sugar
  1 to 2 teaspoons milk

1 Lightly spoon flour into measuring cup; level off. In large bowl, combine 2 cups flour, 2 tablespoons sugar, salt and yeast; mix well.

2 In small saucepan, combine ¾ cup milk, water and shortening. Heat until very warm (120 to 130°F.). Add warm liquid to flour mixture; blend at low speed until moistened. Beat 3 minutes at medium speed. By hand, stir in remaining ½ to 1 cup flour until dough pulls away from sides of bowl.

3 On lightly floured surface, knead dough until smooth and elastic, about 5 minutes. Place dough in greased bowl. Cover loosely with greased plastic wrap and cloth towel. Let rise in warm place (80 to 85°F.) until light and doubled in size, 45 to 60 minutes.

4 Grease 12-inch pizza pan or large cookie sheet. In shallow dish or pie pan, combine nuts, ½ cup sugar, brown sugar and cinnamon; mix well. Place melted butter in another shallow dish or pie pan.

continued on p. 16

COOK'S NOTES

Recipe Fact
Grace Autrey of Denver, Colorado, created this cinnamon-crusted coffee cake for the 9th BAKE-OFF® Contest.

Kitchen Tip
Yeast doughs need to rise in a warm spot where the temperature is between 80 and 85°F. To create a warm place, try one of these methods:

1. Set the oven to 400°F. Turn the oven on for 1 minute, then turn it off. Place the covered bowl of dough on the center rack of the oven and close the door. Leave the dough in the warmed oven until it has doubled.

2. Place the covered bowl of dough on a wire rack over a pan of hot water in a draft-free spot. If the water cools before the dough has risen completely, exchange it with hot water.

Make-Ahead Tip

To make this coffee cake ahead, prepare and bake the cake, but do not glaze it. Tightly wrap the cooled cake in foil and freeze it for up to 3 months. To thaw, loosen the foil and leave the cake at room temperature for 2 to 3 hours. Just before serving, warm the cake and glaze it.

Serving Suggestion

Cut the coffee cake into wedges to serve it. Enjoy it with a fruit-flavored tea or café au lait.

5 Punch down dough several times to remove all air bubbles. Turn dough out onto lightly floured surface. Pinch off a 1½ to 2-inch piece of dough; roll into 6×½-inch strip. Repeat with remaining dough. Dip each dough strip in butter to coat; roll in sugar mixture to coat evenly. Place 1 strip in center of pan; wind to form a coil. Repeat with remaining strips, placing close together to make a round, flat coffee cake. Cover; let rise in warm place until light and doubled in size, 45 to 60 minutes.

6 Heat oven to 350°F. Uncover coffee cake. Bake 20 to 25 minutes or until golden brown. Cool 5 minutes. Carefully remove from pan; place on serving plate.

7 In small bowl, combine glaze ingredients, adding enough milk for desired drizzling consistency. Drizzle over warm coffee cake.

16 servings

HIGH ALTITUDE (ABOVE 3500 FEET): No change.

NUTRITION INFORMATION PER SERVING:

SERVING SIZE: 1/16 of Recipe

Calories		240	Calories from Fat	100
			% DAILY VALUE	
Total Fat	11	g	17%	
Saturated	4	g	20%	
Cholesterol	15	mg	5%	
Sodium	200	mg	8%	
Total Carbohydrate	32	g	11%	
Dietary Fiber	1	g	4%	
Sugars	14	g		
Protein	3	g		
Vitamin A	4%		Vitamin C	0%
Calcium	0%		Iron	8%

DIETARY EXCHANGES: 1 Starch, 1 Fruit, 2 Fat
OR 2 Carbohydrate, 2 Fat

California Casserole

Pictured on right

Prep Time: 1 hour (Ready in 1 hour 25 minutes)

Recipe Fact
Margaret Hatheway's Grand Prize winnings for the 8th BAKE-OFF® Contest sent her on a cook's tour abroad. She introduced this most American of dishes to chefs all across Europe.

Ingredient Substitution
Boneless pork, cut into 1-inch pieces, can be used in place of the veal in this casserole.

Healthy Hint
This hearty main dish is equally delicious without the sauce. Serving the casserole plain reduces the amount of fat in each serving by about 7 grams. Eliminating the sauce makes the recipe quicker, too.

CASSEROLE
⅓ cup Pillsbury BEST® All Purpose Flour
1 teaspoon paprika
2 lb. boneless veal, cut into 1-inch pieces
¼ cup oil
½ teaspoon salt
⅛ teaspoon pepper
1 cup water
1 (10¾-oz.) can condensed cream of chicken soup
1½ cups water
1 (16-oz.) jar (1½ cups) small onions, drained

DUMPLINGS
2 cups Pillsbury BEST® All Purpose Flour
4 teaspoons baking powder
1 tablespoon poppy seed, if desired
1 teaspoon instant minced onion
1 teaspoon celery seed
1 teaspoon poultry seasoning
¼ teaspoon salt
¼ cup oil
¾ to 1 cup milk
2 tablespoons margarine or butter, melted
½ cup Progresso® Plain Bread Crumbs

SAUCE
1 (10¾-oz.) can condensed cream of chicken soup
1 (8-oz.) container sour cream
¼ cup milk

1 In small bowl or plastic food storage bag, combine ⅓ cup flour and paprika; mix or shake well. Add veal; coat well with flour mixture.

2 In 12-inch skillet, heat ¼ cup oil over medium-high heat until hot. Add veal; cook until browned. Add ½ teaspoon salt, pepper and 1 cup water. Bring to a boil. Reduce heat; simmer uncovered 30 minutes or until veal is tender, stirring occasionally. Transfer veal mixture to ungreased 13×9-inch (3-quart) baking dish or 3-quart casserole.

3 In same skillet, combine 1 can cream of chicken soup and 1½ cups water; blend well. Bring to a boil, stirring constantly. Pour over veal mixture in baking dish. Add onions; mix well.

4 Heat oven to 425°F. Lightly spoon flour into measuring cup; level off. In large bowl, combine 2 cups flour, baking powder, poppy seed, minced onion, celery seed, poultry seasoning and ¼ teaspoon salt; mix well. Add ¼ cup oil and enough milk so that, when stirred, dry ingredients are just moistened.

5 In small bowl, combine margarine and bread crumbs; mix well. Drop rounded tablespoons of dough into crumb mixture; roll to coat well. Arrange dumplings over warm veal mixture. Bake at 425°F. for 20 to 25 minutes or until dumplings are deep golden brown.

6 Meanwhile, in medium saucepan, combine all sauce ingredients; blend well. Bring just to a boil. Reduce heat; simmer 2 to 3 minutes or until thoroughly heated, stirring frequently. Serve sauce with casserole and dumplings.

10 servings

HIGH ALTITUDE (ABOVE 3500 FEET): No change.

NUTRITION INFORMATION PER SERVING:

SERVING SIZE:	1/10 of Recipe		
Calories	530	Calories from Fat	270
		% DAILY VALUE	
Total Fat	30 g	46%	
Saturated	8 g	40%	
Cholesterol	75 mg	25%	
Sodium	1060 mg	44%	
Total Carbohydrate	42 g	14%	
Dietary Fiber	2 g	8%	
Sugars	5 g		
Protein	23 g		
Vitamin A	15%	Vitamin C	4%
Calcium	25%	Iron	20%

DIETARY EXCHANGES: 3 Starch, 2 Lean Meat, 4 Fat
OR 3 Carbohydrate, 2 Lean Meat, 4 Fat

Kitchen Tip

For best baking results, be sure the casserole mixture is warm when you top it with the dumplings.

Serving Suggestion

Enjoy this casserole with a crisp green salad tossed with a vinaigrette dressing.

Streamlining the '60s

*L*ifestyles changed dramatically in the 1960s. There were more single parent families, many women entered the workforce and time became more precious, especially for preparing meals. Consequently, working women wanted help and eagerly chose convenience foods and time-saving appliances.

In 1966, Pillsbury's "Busy Lady" theme featured simplified recipes. Convenience products such as refrigerated doughs, cake mixes, canned meats, frozen vegetables and processed cheeses appeared in BAKE-OFF® recipes. The 1969 BAKE-OFF® Contest marked the first time a recipe made with refrigerated dough won the Grand Prize.

1. **Leona Schnuelle**, Crab Orchard, Neb., hears from Sally Pillsbury about the exciting upcoming events at the 12th BAKE-OFF® Contest. Later Leona would become the Grand Prize Winner.

2. **Linda Watczak**, Duluth, Minn., was a BAKE-OFF® finalist in 1967 when the contest was tagged with the "Busy Lady" theme to reflect the changing lifestyle in America.

3. Winning prize money is an added benefit for a finalist like **Lousie A. Schlinkert**, China Lake, Calif., but the real thrill, according to most contestants, is simply becoming a BAKE-OFF® finalist.

4. With food paparazzi all around, finalist **Frayda Kahn** graciously displays her cooking skills.

COOK'S NOTES

Recipe Fact
Betty Taylor of Dallas, Texas, left the 19th contest $5,000 richer after entering this unique lasagna recipe.

Kitchen Tip
To reheat this lasagna, wrap it loosely in foil and heat at 375°F. for 20 to 25 minutes.

Just for Kids
Kids will like this fun and easy recipe for lasagna. Serve it with fresh fruit and *Funfetti Cookies* *p. 87.*

Serving Suggestion
A crisp green salad goes well with this bread-topped lasagna. Serve *Kentucky Butter Cake* *p. 33* as the sweet finale.

Crafty Crescent Lasagna

Pictured on right

Prep Time: 30 minutes (Ready in 55 minutes)

MEAT FILLING
- **½ lb. bulk pork sausage**
- **½ lb. ground beef**
- **¾ cup chopped onions**
- **1 tablespoon dried parsley flakes**
- **½ teaspoon dried basil leaves**
- **½ teaspoon dried oregano leaves**
- **1 small garlic clove, minced**
- **Dash pepper**
- **1 (6-oz.) can tomato paste**

CHEESE FILLING
- **¼ cup grated Parmesan cheese**
- **1 cup small curd cottage cheese**
- **1 egg**

CRUST
- **2 (8-oz.) cans Pillsbury Refrigerated Crescent Dinner Rolls**
- **2 (7×4-inch) slices mozzarella cheese**
- **1 tablespoon milk**
- **1 tablespoon sesame seed**

1 In large skillet, brown sausage and ground beef until thoroughly cooked. Drain. Stir in all remaining meat filling ingredients; simmer 5 minutes, stirring occasionally.

2 Heat oven to 375°F. In small bowl, combine all cheese filling ingredients; blend well. Unroll dough into 4 long rectangles. Place dough crosswise, side by side, on ungreased cookie sheet; firmly press edges and perforations to seal. Press to form 15×13-inch rectangle.

3 Spoon half of meat filling in 6-inch strip lengthwise down center of dough to within 1 inch of short sides. Spoon cheese filling over meat mixture; spoon remaining meat mixture evenly over cheese mixture. Arrange mozzarella cheese slices over meat filling. Fold short sides of dough 1 inch over filling. Fold long sides of dough tightly over filling, overlapping edges in center ¼ inch; firmly pinch center seam and ends to seal. Brush with milk; sprinkle with sesame seed.

4 Bake at 375°F. for 23 to 27 minutes or until deep golden brown.

8 servings

NUTRITION INFORMATION PER SERVING:
SERVING SIZE: 1/8 of Recipe

Calories	420	Calories from Fat	220
		% DAILY VALUE	
Total Fat	24 g	37%	
Saturated	8 g	40%	
Cholesterol	65 mg	22%	
Sodium	1030 mg	43%	
Total Carbohydrate	30 g	10%	
Dietary Fiber	2 g	8%	
Sugars	6 g		
Protein	21 g		
Vitamin A	15%	Vitamin C	10%
Calcium	20%	Iron	15%

DIETARY EXCHANGES: 2 Starch, 2 High-Fat Meat, 1-1/2 Fat
OR 2 Carbohydrate, 2 High-Fat Meat, 1-1/2 Fat

From top:
Kentucky Butter Cake p. 34,
Crafty Crescent Lasagna

Poppin' Fresh Barbecups

Pictured on left

Prep Time: 20 minutes (Ready in 35 minutes)

1 lb. ground beef
½ cup barbecue sauce
1 tablespoon instant minced onion or
    ¼ cup chopped onion
1 to 2 tablespoons brown sugar
1 (12-oz.) can Hungry Jack® Refrigerated
    Flaky Biscuits
2 oz. (½ cup) shredded Cheddar or
    American cheese

1 Heat oven to 400°F. Grease 10 muffin cups. In large skillet, brown ground beef until thoroughly cooked. Drain. Stir in barbecue sauce, onion and brown sugar. Cook 1 minute to blend flavors, stirring constantly.

2 Separate dough into 10 biscuits. Place 1 biscuit in each greased muffin cup; firmly press in bottom and up sides, forming ¼-inch rim. Spoon about ¼ cup beef mixture into each biscuit-lined cup. Sprinkle each with cheese.

3 Bake at 400°F. for 10 to 12 minutes or until edges of biscuits are golden brown. Cool 1 minute; remove from pan.

10 servings

NUTRITION INFORMATION PER SERVING:
SERVING SIZE: 1/10 of Recipe

Calories	240	Calories from Fat	120
		% DAILY VALUE	
Total Fat	13 g	20%	
Saturated	5 g	25%	
Cholesterol	35 mg	12%	
Sodium	520 mg	22%	
Total Carbohydrate	19 g	6%	
Dietary Fiber	1 g	3%	
Sugars	5 g		
Protein	11 g		
Vitamin A	4%	Vitamin C	0%
Calcium	6%	Iron	10%

DIETARY EXCHANGES: 1 Starch, 1/2 Fruit, 1 Medium-Fat Meat, 1-1/2 Fat **OR** 1-1/2 Carbohydrate, 1 Medium-Fat Meat, 1-1/2 Fat

COOK'S NOTES

Recipe Fact

This all-time favorite recipe was entered in the 19th contest by 12-year-old Peter Russell of Shawnee-Mission, Kansas. He created this easy recipe for dinner one night when his mom and dad were working late.

Ingredient Substitution

Use your favorite barbecue sauce in this recipe, or experiment with a new flavor.

Make-Ahead Tip

Assemble the recipe; cover and refrigerate up to 2 hours. Bake it as directed until the biscuits are golden, adding a few extra minutes if necessary.

Hungry Boys' Casserole

Pictured on right

Prep Time: 40 minutes (Ready in 1 hour 5 minutes)

Recipe Fact
This Grand Prize-winning casserole was created by Mira Walilko of Detroit, Michigan, for the 15th BAKE-OFF® Contest.

Ingredient Substitutions
One 15-ounce can of lima beans, drained, can be used in place of the garbanzo beans.

Instead of mixing the biscuits from scratch, try using one 12-ounce can of Hungry Jack® Refrigerated Buttermilk Flaky Biscuits. Cut 1-inch rounds from center of each biscuit and reserve. Assemble the casserole and biscuits as directed in the recipe. Bake at 400°F. for 11 to 13 minutes or until biscuits are golden brown.

CASSEROLE
1½ lb. ground beef
1 cup chopped celery
½ cup chopped onion
½ cup chopped green bell pepper
1 garlic clove, minced
1 (6-oz.) can tomato paste
¾ cup water
1 teaspoon paprika
½ teaspoon salt
1 (16-oz.) can baked beans, undrained
1 (15-oz.) can Green Giant® or Old El Paso® Garbanzo Beans or Progresso® Chick Peas, drained

BISCUITS
1½ cups Pillsbury BEST® All Purpose Flour
2 teaspoons baking powder
½ teaspoon salt
¼ cup margarine or butter
½ to ¾ cup milk
2 tablespoons sliced stuffed green olives
1 tablespoon slivered almonds

1 In 12-inch skillet, combine ground beef, celery, onion, bell pepper and garlic. Cook over medium-high heat until beef is browned and thoroughly cooked and vegetables are crisp-tender. Drain. Reduce heat to low. Stir in tomato paste, water, paprika and ½ teaspoon salt. Add baked beans and garbanzo beans; simmer while preparing biscuits, stirring occasionally.

2 Heat oven to 425°F. Lightly spoon flour into measuring cup; level off. In large bowl, combine flour, baking powder and ½ teaspoon salt; mix well. With pastry blender or fork, cut in margarine until mixture resembles coarse crumbs. Gradually stir in enough milk until mixture leaves sides of bowl and forms a soft, moist dough.

3 On floured surface, gently knead dough 8 times. Roll dough to ¼-inch thickness. Cut with floured 2½-inch doughnut cutter. Reserve dough centers. Reroll dough to cut additional biscuits.

4 Reserve ½ cup of beef mixture. Pour remaining hot beef mixture into ungreased 13×9-inch (3-quart) baking dish. Arrange biscuits without centers over hot beef mixture. Stir olives and almonds into reserved ½ cup beef mixture; spoon into center of each biscuit. Top each with biscuit centers.

5 Bake at 425°F. for 15 to 25 minutes or until biscuits are golden brown.

8 servings

HIGH ALTITUDE (ABOVE 3500 FEET): No change.

NUTRITION INFORMATION PER SERVING:
SERVING SIZE: 1/8 of Recipe

Calories	470	Calories from Fat	200
		% DAILY VALUE	
Total Fat	22 g	34%	
Saturated	7 g	35%	
Cholesterol	55 mg	18%	
Sodium	1000 mg	42%	
Total Carbohydrate	44 g	15%	
Dietary Fiber	8 g	32%	
Sugars	3 g		
Protein	23 g		
Vitamin A	20%	Vitamin C	20%
Calcium	15%	Iron	25%

DIETARY EXCHANGES: 3 Starch, 2 Medium-Fat Meat, 2 Fat
OR 3 Carbohydrate, 2 Medium-Fat Meat, 2 Fat

Swiss Ham Ring-Around

Pictured on left

Prep Time: 20 minutes (Ready in 50 minutes)

1 tablespoon butter, softened
¼ cup chopped fresh parsley or
    2 tablespoons dried parsley flakes
2 tablespoons finely chopped onion or
    1½ teaspoons instant minced onion
2 tablespoons prepared mustard
1 teaspoon lemon juice
6 oz. (1½ cups) shredded Swiss cheese
1 cup chopped fresh broccoli or Green Giant®
    Frozen Chopped Broccoli, cooked, drained
1 cup (6 oz.) diced cooked ham
1 (8-oz.) can Pillsbury Refrigerated Crescent
    Dinner Rolls

1 Heat oven to 350° F. Grease large cookie sheet. In large bowl, combine butter, parsley, onion, mustard and lemon juice; blend well. Add cheese, cooked broccoli and ham; mix lightly. Set aside.

2 Unroll dough into 8 triangles. Arrange triangles on greased cookie sheet with shortest sides toward center, overlapping in wreath shape and leaving a 3-inch round opening in center (see diagram).

3 Spoon ham filling on widest part of dough. Pull end points of triangles over filling and tuck under dough to form a ring.

4 Bake at 350°F. for 25 to 30 minutes or until golden brown.

8 servings

NUTRITION INFORMATION PER SERVING:
SERVING SIZE: 1/8 of Recipe

Calories	230	Calories from Fat	130
		% DAILY VALUE	
Total Fat	14 g	22%	
Saturated	7 g	35%	
Cholesterol	35 mg	12%	
Sodium	640 mg	27%	
Total Carbohydrate	13 g	4%	
Dietary Fiber	1 g	3%	
Sugars	2 g		
Protein	12 g		
Vitamin A	10%	Vitamin C	15%
Calcium	20%	Iron	6%

DIETARY EXCHANGES: 1 Starch, 1-1/2 Medium-Fat Meat, 1 Fat **OR** 1 Carbohydrate, 1-1/2 Medium-Fat Meat, 1 Fat

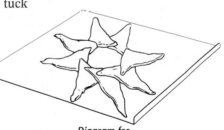

*Diagram for
Swiss Ham Ring-Around*

Magic Marshmallow Crescent Puffs

Pictured on right

Prep Time: 20 minutes (Ready in 35 minutes)

Recipe Fact

Edna (Holmgren) Walker of Hopkins, Minnesota entered this sweet treat in 1969 and won the Grand Prize. That year marked the first BAKE-OFF® Contest in which a recipe made with refrigerated prepared dough won top honors.

The marshmallow in each puff melts during baking, creating a sweet, syrupy, hollow center.

Kitchen Tips

For best results, be sure to use refrigerated dough products by the "use before" date stamped on the end of the can. Store prepared dough in the coolest part of the refrigerator.

Use a large curved spoon to easily remove the puffs from the muffin cups.

PUFFS
¼ **cup sugar**
2 tablespoons Pillsbury BEST® All Purpose Flour
1 teaspoon cinnamon
2 (8-oz.) cans Pillsbury Refrigerated Crescent Dinner Rolls
16 large marshmallows
¼ **cup margarine or butter, melted**

GLAZE
½ **cup powdered sugar**
½ **teaspoon vanilla**
2 to 3 teaspoons milk
¼ **cup chopped nuts, if desired**

1 Heat oven to 375°F. Spray 16 muffin cups with nonstick cooking spray. In small bowl, combine sugar, flour and cinnamon; mix well.

2 Separate dough into 16 triangles. Dip 1 marshmallow in margarine; roll in sugar mixture. Place marshmallow on shortest side of triangle. Roll up starting at shortest side of triangle and rolling to opposite point. Completely cover marshmallow with dough; firmly pinch edges to seal. Dip 1 end in remaining margarine; place margarine side down in sprayed muffin cup. Repeat with remaining marshmallows.

3 Bake at 375°F. for 12 to 15 minutes or until golden brown. (Place foil or cookie sheet on rack below muffin cups to guard against spills.) Remove from oven; cool 1 minute. Remove from muffin cups; place on wire racks set over waxed paper.

4 In small bowl, blend powdered sugar, vanilla and enough milk for desired drizzling consistency. Drizzle over warm rolls. Sprinkle with nuts.

16 rolls

NUTRITION INFORMATION PER SERVING:
SERVING SIZE: 1 Roll

Calories	200	Calories from Fat	90
		% DAILY VALUE	
Total Fat	10 g	15%	
Saturated	2 g	10%	
Cholesterol	0 mg	0%	
Sodium	250 mg	10%	
Total Carbohydrate	25 g	8%	
Dietary Fiber	1 g	2%	
Sugars	13 g		
Protein	2 g		
Vitamin A	2%	Vitamin C	0%
Calcium	0%	Iron	4%

DIETARY EXCHANGES: 1/2 Starch, 1 Fruit, 2 Fat
OR 1-1/2 Carbohydrate, 2 Fat

Tunnel of Fudge Cake

Pictured on right and on cover

Prep Time: 40 minutes (Ready in 4 hours 10 minutes)

Recipe Facts

This well-known BAKE-OFF® cake was created by Ella Helfrich of Houston, Texas. The original recipe used a frosting mix that is no longer available. Our updated version for this 50th anniversary issue uses milk, pudding mix and chocolate chips in place of the frosting mix.

The popularity of Bundt® fluted tube pans increased after this recipe won the judges' approval in the 17th contest. Only one company manufactured Bundt® pans back then, and the factory went on a 24-hour production schedule to keep up with the demand.

Ingredient Info

The 2 cups of nuts in this cake are essential for the success of this recipe. They help absorb moisture and contribute to the volume of the cake.

FILLING
- 1½ cups milk
- 1 (3.4-oz.) pkg. chocolate fudge pudding and pie filling mix (not instant)
- 1 (6-oz.) pkg. (1 cup) semi-sweet chocolate chips

CAKE
- 1⅓ cups sugar
- ¾ cup butter, softened
- ½ cup shortening
- 1 teaspoon vanilla
- 4 eggs
- 2 cups Pillsbury BEST® All Purpose Flour
- ½ cup unsweetened cocoa
- ½ teaspoon baking powder
- ½ teaspoon salt
- 1 cup milk
- 2 cups chopped walnuts

GLAZE
- ¾ cup powdered sugar
- ¼ cup unsweetened cocoa
- 4 to 6 teaspoons milk

1 In medium saucepan, combine 1½ cups milk and pudding mix; cook as directed on package. Add chocolate chips; stir until melted. Set aside.

2 Heat oven to 350°F. Grease and flour 12-cup Bundt® pan or 10-inch tube pan. In large bowl, combine sugar, butter and shortening; beat until light and fluffy. Add vanilla and eggs; mix well.

3 Lightly spoon flour into measuring cup; level off. Add flour, ½ cup cocoa, baking powder, salt and 1 cup milk; beat at low speed until moistened. Beat 3 minutes at medium speed. Stir in walnuts.

4 Reserve 2 cups of the batter. Pour remaining batter into greased and floured pan. Spoon filling in ring on top of batter, making sure it does not touch sides of pan. Spoon reserved batter over filling.

5 Bake at 350°F. for 50 to 60 minutes or until cake springs back when touched lightly in center. Cool 1 hour; remove from pan. Cool 1½ hours or until completely cooled.

6 In small bowl, blend all glaze ingredients, adding enough milk for desired drizzling consistency. Spoon over top of cake, allowing some to run down sides. Use very sharp or serrated knife to slice cake. Best when served same day; store any remaining cake in refrigerator.

16 servings

HIGH ALTITUDE (ABOVE 3500 FEET):
Decrease sugar to 1 cup; increase flour to 2¼ cups. Bake as directed above.

Kitchen Tip

To easily grease and flour baking pans in one step, mix 2 parts shortening to 1 part flour. Keep this mixture in a covered container and apply it to the pan when the recipe requires a greased and floured surface.

NUTRITION INFORMATION PER SERVING:

SERVING SIZE:	1/16 of Recipe		
Calories	570	Calories from Fat	270
		% DAILY VALUE	
Total Fat	30 g	46%	
Saturated	11 g	55%	
Cholesterol	80 mg	27%	
Sodium	230 mg	10%	
Total Carbohydrate	68 g	23%	
Dietary Fiber	3 g	12%	
Sugars	49 g		
Protein	8 g		
Vitamin A	10%	Vitamin C	0%
Calcium	10%	Iron	15%

DIETARY EXCHANGES: 2-1/2 Starch, 2 Fruit, 5-1/2 Fat
OR 4-1/2 Carbohydrate, 5-1/2 Fat

Kentucky Butter Cake

Pictured on page 23

Prep Time: 20 minutes (Ready in 3 hours 10 minutes)

Pictured on page 23

Recipe Fact

Pound cake derives its name from the original recipe, which called for one pound each of butter, sugar, flour and eggs. This ratio of ingredients produces a dense, moist cake with a fine crumb and rich, full flavor. Traditionally, pound cake is flavored with vanilla or lemon. Nell Lewis of Platte City, Missouri, attended the 15th BAKE-OFF® Contest with this creative recipe for buttermilk pound cake infused with a warm butter sauce.

Ingredient Substitution

Sour milk can be used in place of the buttermilk in this pound cake. To make milk sour, place 1 tablespoon of lemon juice or white vinegar in a measuring cup, then add enough milk to equal 1 cup. Stir mixture and let stand until slightly thickened.

CAKE
2 cups sugar
1 cup butter, softened
2 teaspoons vanilla or rum extract
4 eggs
3 cups Pillsbury BEST® All Purpose Flour
1 teaspoon salt
1 teaspoon baking powder
½ teaspoon baking soda
1 cup buttermilk

SAUCE
¾ cup sugar
⅓ cup butter
3 tablespoons water
1 to 2 teaspoons vanilla or rum extract

GARNISH
2 to 3 teaspoons powdered sugar

1 Heat oven to 325°F. Generously grease and lightly flour 12-cup Bundt® pan or 10-inch tube pan. In large bowl, combine 2 cups sugar and 1 cup butter; beat well. Add vanilla and eggs; blend well. Lightly spoon flour into measuring cup; level off. Add flour and all remaining cake ingredients; blend at low speed until moistened. Beat 3 minutes at medium speed. Pour batter into greased and floured pan.

2 Bake at 325°F. for 55 to 70 minutes or until toothpick inserted in center comes out clean.

3 In small saucepan, combine all sauce ingredients; cook over low heat, stirring occasionally, until butter melts. DO NOT BOIL. With long-tined fork, pierce cake 10 to 12 times. Slowly pour hot sauce over warm cake. Let stand 5 to 10 minutes or until sauce is absorbed.

4 Invert cake onto serving plate. Cool 1½ hours or until completely cooled. Just before serving, sprinkle with powdered sugar. If desired, serve with whipped cream.

12 servings

HIGH ALTITUDE (ABOVE 3500 FEET): Decrease sugar in cake to 1¾ cups; increase buttermilk to 1 cup plus 2 tablespoons. Bake at 350°F. for 60 to 70 minutes.

NUTRITION INFORMATION PER SERVING:
SERVING SIZE: 1/12 of Recipe

Calories	520	Calories from Fat	210
		% DAILY VALUE	
Total Fat	23 g	35%	
Saturated	13 g	65%	
Cholesterol	125 mg	42%	
Sodium	520 mg	22%	
Total Carbohydrate	72 g	24%	
Dietary Fiber	1 g	3%	
Sugars	48 g		
Protein	6 g		
Vitamin A	20%	Vitamin C	0%
Calcium	6%	Iron	10%

DIETARY EXCHANGES: 2 Starch, 3 Fruit, 4 Fat
OR 5 Carbohydrate, 4 Fat

Oatmeal Carmelitas

Pictured on page 39

Prep Time: 30 minutes (Ready in 2 hours 55 minutes)

CRUST
2 cups Pillsbury BEST® All Purpose Flour
2 cups quick-cooking rolled oats
1½ cups firmly packed brown sugar
1 teaspoon baking soda
½ teaspoon salt
1¼ cups margarine or butter, softened

FILLING
1 (12.5-oz.) jar (1 cup) caramel ice cream topping
3 tablespoons Pillsbury BEST® All Purpose Flour
1 (6-oz.) pkg. (1 cup) semi-sweet chocolate chips
½ cup chopped nuts

1 Heat oven to 350°F. Grease 13×9-inch pan. Lightly spoon flour into measuring cup; level off. In large bowl, combine all crust ingredients; mix at low speed until crumbly. Reserve half of crumb mixture (about 3 cups) for topping. Press remaining crumb mixture in bottom of greased pan. Bake at 350°F. for 10 minutes.

2 Meanwhile, in small bowl, combine caramel topping and 3 tablespoons flour; blend well.

3 Remove partially baked crust from oven; sprinkle with chocolate chips and nuts. Drizzle evenly with caramel mixture; sprinkle with reserved crumb mixture.

4 Return to oven; bake an additional 18 to 22 minutes or until golden brown. Cool 1 hour or until completely cooled. Refrigerate 1 to 2 hours or until filling is set. Cut into bars.

36 bars

HIGH ALTITUDE (ABOVE 3500 FEET): No change.

NUTRITION INFORMATION PER SERVING:

SERVING SIZE:	1 Bar		
Calories	200	Calories from Fat	80
		% DAILY VALUE	
Total Fat	9 g	14%	
Saturated	2 g	10%	
Cholesterol	0 mg	0%	
Sodium	180 mg	8%	
Total Carbohydrate	28 g	9%	
Dietary Fiber	1 g	4%	
Sugars	17 g		
Protein	2 g		
Vitamin A	6%	Vitamin C	0%
Calcium	2%	Iron	6%

DIETARY EXCHANGES: 1 Starch, 1 Fruit, 1-1/2 Fat
OR 2 Carbohydrate, 1-1/2 Fat

COOK'S NOTES

Recipe Fact
"Busy Lady" was the theme for the 18th contest, held in 1967. These bars, created by Erlyce Larson of Kennedy, Minnesota, have become a favorite. Her recipe is one of the most requested recipes ever.

Kitchen Tip
Lining the pan with foil makes it simple to remove the bars from the pan and cut them. Turn the pan over and mold the foil over the bottom of the pan. Then fit it easily into the pan and grease the foil. Be sure to cut the sheet of foil long enough so that you'll be able to grasp the extra foil and lift out the bars.

Storage Tip
To keep these bars soft and delicious, store them in a tightly covered container.

Mystery Pecan Pie

Pictured on right

Prep Time: 15 minutes (Ready in 3 hours)

Recipe Fact
The prize for this pie, entered in the 16th contest by Mary McClain of North Little Rock, Arkansas, was $1,000. We've simplified her recipe by using Pillsbury Refrigerated Pie Crust.

Ingredient Info
Either light or dark corn syrup can be used in this recipe. Dark corn syrup will have a stronger flavor and give the pie a darker color.

Kitchen Tip
It's easy to make a foil protector to prevent the pie crust edge from over-browning. First, cut a 12-inch wide piece of foil four inches longer than the diameter of the pie pan. Then cut a circle from the center of the foil that is two inches smaller than the diameter of the pie pan. Center the foil over the partially baked pie and gently fold it around the crust edge.

CRUST
  1 Pillsbury Refrigerated Pie Crust (from 15-oz. pkg.)
FILLING
  1 (8-oz.) pkg. cream cheese, softened
  ⅓ cup sugar
  ¼ teaspoon salt
  1 teaspoon vanilla
  1 egg
  3 eggs
  ¼ cup sugar
  1 cup corn syrup
  1 teaspoon vanilla
  1¼ cups chopped pecans

1 Prepare pie crust as directed on package for *one-crust filled pie* using 9-inch pie pan.

2 Heat oven to 375°F. In small bowl, combine cream cheese, ⅓ cup sugar, salt, 1 teaspoon vanilla and 1 egg; beat at low speed until smooth and well blended. Set aside.

3 In another small bowl, beat 3 eggs. Add ¼ cup sugar, corn syrup and 1 teaspoon vanilla; blend well. Spread cream cheese mixture in bottom of crust-lined pan. Sprinkle with pecans. Gently pour corn syrup mixture over pecans.

4 Bake at 375°F. for 35 to 45 minutes or until center is set. If necessary, cover edge of pie crust with foil after 15 to 20 minutes of baking to prevent excessive browning. Cool 2 hours or until completely cooled. Store in refrigerator.

8 servings

NUTRITION INFORMATION PER SERVING:
SERVING SIZE: 1/8 of Recipe

Calories	560	Calories from Fat	280
		% DAILY VALUE	
Total Fat	31 g	48%	
Saturated	11 g	55%	
Cholesterol	145 mg	48%	
Sodium	330 mg	14%	
Total Carbohydrate	64 g	21%	
Dietary Fiber	2 g	8%	
Sugars	32 g		
Protein	7 g		
Vitamin A	10%	Vitamin C	0%
Calcium	4%	Iron	8%

DIETARY EXCHANGES: 1 Starch, 3-1/2 Fruit, 1/2 High-Fat Meat, 5 Fat **OR** 4-1/2 Carbohydrate, 1/2 High-Fat Meat, 5 Fat

Candy Bar Cookies

Pictured on right

Prep Time: 1 hour 15 minutes (Ready in 2 hours 15 minutes)

Recipe Fact
At the 13th contest, Alice Reese of Minneapolis, Minnesota, won top honors for this spectacular cookie.

Kitchen Tips
Twenty-eight caramels, about 15 ounces, are used in the filling. Look for caramels in the candy or bulk section of the grocery store.

Cut with a fluted pastry wheel, this cookie looks wonderfully elegant. For a special party tray, try cutting diamond shapes or smaller squares.

Make-Ahead Tip
Prepare and bake the base of these cookies up to a month ahead. Wrap them tightly and freeze them until you're ready to complete the recipe.

BASE
¾ **cup powdered sugar**
¾ **cup margarine or butter, softened**
2 **tablespoons whipping cream**
1 **teaspoon vanilla**
2 **cups Pillsbury BEST® All Purpose Flour**

FILLING
28 **caramels, unwrapped**
¼ **cup whipping cream**
¼ **cup margarine or butter**
1 **cup powdered sugar**
1 **cup chopped pecans**

GLAZE
½ **cup semi-sweet chocolate chips**
2 **tablespoons whipping cream**
1 **tablespoon margarine or butter**
¼ **cup powdered sugar**
1 **teaspoon vanilla**
48 **pecan halves (⅔ cup), if desired**

1 In large bowl, combine all base ingredients except flour; blend well. Lightly spoon flour into measuring cup; level off. Stir in flour; mix well. If necessary, cover with plastic wrap; refrigerate 1 hour for easier handling.

2 Heat oven to 325°F. Divide dough in half. On well-floured surface, roll each half of dough into 12×8-inch rectangle. With pastry wheel or knife, cut into 2-inch squares. Place ½ inch apart on ungreased cookie sheets.

3 Bake at 325°F. for 12 to 16 minutes or until set. Remove from cookie sheets; cool on wire racks.

4 In medium saucepan, combine caramels, ¼ cup whipping cream and ¼ cup margarine; cook over low heat, stirring frequently, until caramels are melted and mixture is smooth. Remove from heat; stir in 1 cup powdered sugar and chopped pecans. (Add additional whipping cream a few drops at a time, if needed for desired spreading consistency.) Spread 1 teaspoon warm filling on each cookie square.

5 In small saucepan, combine chocolate chips, 2 tablespoons whipping cream and 1 tablespoon margarine; cook over low heat, stirring frequently, until chocolate chips are melted and mixture is smooth. Remove from heat; stir in ¼ cup powdered sugar and 1 teaspoon vanilla. Spread glaze evenly over caramel filling on each cookie. Top each with pecan half.

4 dozen cookies

HIGH ALTITUDE (ABOVE 3500 FEET): No change.

From top:
Oatmeal Carmelitas p. 35,
Candy Bar Cookies

Cheese-Crusted Flat Bread

Pictured on right

Prep Time: 20 minutes (Ready in 2 hours)

2½ to 3 cups Pillsbury BEST® All Purpose Flour
1 tablespoon sugar
1 teaspoon salt
1 pkg. active dry yeast
¾ cup milk
¼ cup water
2 tablespoons butter
2 tablespoons chopped onion
¼ cup butter, melted
½ teaspoon dried oregano leaves
½ teaspoon paprika
¼ teaspoon garlic salt
¼ teaspoon celery seed
4 oz. (1 cup) shredded Cheddar cheese

1 Lightly spoon flour into measuring cup; level off. In large bowl, combine 2 cups flour, sugar, salt and yeast; mix well.

2 In small saucepan, combine milk, water and 2 tablespoons butter. Heat until very warm (120 to 130°F.). Add warm liquid to flour mixture; mix well. Stir in remaining ½ to 1 cup flour to form a stiff dough.

3 On lightly floured surface, knead until smooth, about 5 minutes. Place dough in greased bowl. Cover loosely with greased plastic wrap and cloth towel. Let rise in warm place (80 to 85°F.) until light and doubled in size, 45 to 60 minutes.

4 Grease two 9-inch round cake or pie pans. Divide dough in half; press each half in greased pan. In small bowl, combine onion, ¼ cup butter, oregano, paprika, garlic salt and celery seed; mix well. Spread mixture over dough. Prick tops generously with fork. Sprinkle evenly with cheese. Cover; let rise in warm place until light and doubled in size, 30 to 45 minutes.

5 Heat oven to 375°F. Uncover dough. Bake 20 to 25 minutes or until golden brown. Serve warm.

16 servings

HIGH ALTITUDE (ABOVE 3500 FEET): No change.

NUTRITION INFORMATION PER SERVING:
SERVING SIZE: 1/16 of Recipe

Calories	160	Calories from Fat	60
		% DAILY VALUE	
Total Fat	7 g	11%	
Saturated	4 g	20%	
Cholesterol	20 mg	7%	
Sodium	260 mg	11%	
Total Carbohydrate	20 g	7%	
Dietary Fiber	1 g	3%	
Sugars	2 g		
Protein	5 g		
Vitamin A	6%	Vitamin C	0%
Calcium	8%	Iron	8%

DIETARY EXCHANGES: 1-1/2 Starch, 1 Fat
OR 1-1/2 Carbohydrate, 1 Fat

From top:
Dilly Casserole Bread p. 42,
Cheese-Crusted Flat Bread

Dilly Casserole Bread

Pictured on page 41

Prep Time: 20 minutes (Ready in 3 hours)

Recipe Fact
Leona Schnuelle of Crab Orchard, Nebraska, captured the Grand Prize in 1960 for this delicious and easy yeast bread. The recipe is a favorite of our food editor and her family.

Ingredient Info
Dill seed is the dried fruit of the dill plant. When the seeds are heated during baking, they release their flavor, which is a bit stronger than the flavor of the feathery dried dill leaves.

Cottage cheese comes in different forms — small curd, medium curd and large curd. Creamed cottage cheese has 4 to 8 percent cream added to it.

2 to 2⅔ cups Pillsbury BEST® All Purpose Flour
2 tablespoons sugar
2 to 3 teaspoons instant minced onion
2 teaspoons dill seed
1 teaspoon salt
¼ teaspoon baking soda
1 pkg. active dry yeast
¼ cup water
1 tablespoon margarine or butter
1 cup small curd creamed cottage cheese
1 egg
2 teaspoons margarine or butter, melted
¼ teaspoon coarse salt, if desired

1️⃣ Lightly spoon flour into measuring cup; level off. In large bowl, combine 1 cup flour, sugar, onion, dill seed, 1 teaspoon salt, baking soda and yeast; mix well.

2️⃣ In small saucepan, heat water, 1 tablespoon margarine and cottage cheese until very warm (120 to 130°F.). Add warm liquid and egg to flour mixture; blend at low speed until moistened. Beat 3 minutes at medium speed.

3️⃣ By hand, stir in remaining 1 to 1⅔ cups flour to form a stiff batter. Cover loosely with greased plastic wrap and cloth towel. Let rise in warm place (80 to 85°F.) until light and doubled in size, 45 to 60 minutes.

4️⃣ Generously grease 1½ or 2-quart casserole. Stir down batter to remove all air bubbles. Turn batter into greased casserole. Cover; let rise in warm place until light and doubled in size, 30 to 45 minutes.

5️⃣ Heat oven to 350°F. Uncover dough. Bake 30 to 40 minutes or until loaf is deep golden brown and sounds hollow when lightly tapped. If necessary, cover with foil to prevent excessive browning. Immediately remove from casserole; place on wire rack. Brush warm loaf with melted margarine; sprinkle with coarse salt. Cool 15 minutes. Serve warm or cool.

1 (18-slice) loaf

FOOD PROCESSOR DIRECTIONS:

1 In small bowl, dissolve yeast in ¼ cup warm water (105 to 115°F.). In food processor bowl with metal blade, combine 2 cups flour, sugar, onion, dill seed, 1 teaspoon salt, baking soda and 1 tablespoon margarine; process 5 seconds. Add cottage cheese and egg; process about 10 seconds or until blended.

2 With machine running, pour yeast mixture through feed tube. Continue processing until blended, about 20 seconds or until mixture pulls away from sides of bowl and forms a ball. (If dough does not form a ball, add additional flour, 1 tablespoon at a time.)

3 Carefully scrape dough from blade and bowl; place in greased bowl. Cover; let rise. Continue as directed above.

HIGH ALTITUDE (ABOVE 3500 FEET):
Bake at 375°F. for 35 to 40 minutes.

NUTRITION INFORMATION PER SERVING:

SERVING SIZE:	1 Slice		
Calories	100	Calories from Fat	20
		% DAILY VALUE	
Total Fat	2 g	3%	
Saturated	1 g	5%	
Cholesterol	15 mg	5%	
Sodium	230 mg	10%	
Total Carbohydrate	16 g	5%	
Dietary Fiber	1 g	3%	
Sugars	2 g		
Protein	4 g		
Vitamin A	0%	Vitamin C	0%
Calcium	0%	Iron	6%

DIETARY EXCHANGES: 1 Starch, 1/2 Fat
OR 1 Carbohydrate, 1/2 Fat

Kitchen Tip

To activate the yeast, the water in this recipe should be between 120 and 130°F. Using an instant-read thermometer is the fastest, simplest way to determine water temperature. Look for an instant-read thermometer in kitchenware stores or the kitchen utensil aisle of the grocery store.

Serving Suggestion

This versatile bread goes well with many dishes. Enjoy it with grilled chicken or steak or serve it as an accompaniment to soup or stew.

1. Winning the Grand Prize is the perfect ending to the competition which has vaulted many people into celebrity status.

2. Pecan pie in a bar shape won the Grand Prize for Pearl Hall, Snohomish, Wash.

3. Center of attention at Pillsbury's 25th BAKE-OFF® Contest was this gorgeous, multi-tiered anniversary cake.

4. Finalists at the 22nd contest in Honolulu are admiring an example of the latest in cooking appliances—a range typical of what they'll use on the BAKE-OFF® floor.

5. As millions look on via network television, Bob Barker surprises Esther Tomich, San Pedro, Calif., with the announcement of her Grand Prize win at the 28th BAKE-OFF® Contest.

Eclectic Tastes of the '70s

*A*mericans created meals with a special flair – from ethnic to super-easy. More affluent, college-educated families entertained at home, serving wines with meals that had a foreign flair. Adventuresome cooks experimented with herbs and spices.

On the other hand, there was a hearty, homespun appeal in foods, reflected in old-fashioned cookie bars and sweet rolls, as well as wholesome breads. BAKE-OFF® finalists used more natural ingredients, including nuts, fruits and vegetables.

As more women – and a growing number of men – had less time to prepare meals, recipes using convenience products continued to be popular. Microwave ovens, food processors and other small kitchen appliances were growing in popularity.

45

COOK'S NOTES

Recipe Fact

At every contest held
during the 1970s, two
recipes were each awarded
a Grand Prize of $25,000.
At the 25th contest in 1974,
Doris Castle of River Forest,
Illinois, won top honors for
these chicken squares.

Savory Crescent
Chicken Squares

Pictured above

Prep Time: 20 minutes (Ready in 50 minutes)

1 (3-oz.) pkg. cream cheese, softened
1 tablespoon margarine or butter, softened
2 cups cubed cooked chicken
1 tablespoon chopped fresh chives or onion
¼ teaspoon salt
⅛ teaspoon pepper
2 tablespoons milk
1 tablespoon chopped pimientos, if desired
1 (8-oz.) can Pillsbury Refrigerated Crescent
    Dinner Rolls
1 tablespoon margarine or butter, melted
¾ cup seasoned croutons, crushed

1 Heat oven to 350°F. In medium bowl, combine
cream cheese and 1 tablespoon softened margarine;
beat until smooth. Add chicken, chives, salt, pepper,
milk and pimientos; mix well.

From left: Savory Crescent Chicken Squares, Rocky Road Fudge Bars p. 58

2 Separate dough into 4 rectangles. Firmly press perforations to seal. Spoon ½ cup chicken mixture onto center of each rectangle. Pull 4 corners of dough to center of chicken mixture; twist firmly. Pinch edges to seal. Place on ungreased cookie sheet. Brush tops of sandwiches with 1 tablespoon melted margarine; sprinkle with crushed croutons.

3 Bake at 350°F. for 25 to 30 minutes or until golden brown.

4 sandwiches

NUTRITION INFORMATION PER SERVING:
SERVING SIZE: 1 Sandwich

Calories	500	Calories from Fat	280
		% DAILY VALUE	
Total Fat	31 g	48%	
Saturated	10 g	50%	
Cholesterol	85 mg	28%	
Sodium	850 mg	35%	
Total Carbohydrate	28 g	9%	
Dietary Fiber	1 g	4%	
Sugars	5 g		
Protein	27 g		
Vitamin A	15%	Vitamin C	4%
Calcium	6%	Iron	15%

DIETARY EXCHANGES: 2 Starch, 3 Lean Meat, 4 Fat
OR 2 Carbohydrate, 3 Lean Meat, 4 Fat

Ingredient Substitutions

Two 5-ounce cans of chunk chicken, drained and flaked, can be used in place of the cubed cooked chicken.

One-third cup of chive-flavored cream cheese can be used in place of the cream cheese and chives.

Lemon Meringue Dessert Squares

Pictured on right

Prep Time: 40 minutes (Ready in 2 hours 40 minutes)

CRUST
- 1 (1 lb. 2.25-oz.) pkg. Pillsbury Moist Supreme® Yellow Cake Mix
- ½ cup margarine or butter
- 1 egg

FILLING
- 1⅓ cups sugar
- ½ cup cornstarch
- Dash salt
- 1¾ cups water
- 4 egg yolks, slightly beaten
- 2 tablespoons margarine or butter
- 2 tablespoons grated lemon peel
- ½ cup lemon juice

MERINGUE
- 4 egg whites
- ¼ teaspoon cream of tartar
- ½ cup sugar

1 Heat oven to 350°F. Grease 13×9-inch pan. In large bowl, combine all crust ingredients; mix at low speed until crumbly. Press mixture in bottom of greased pan.

2 In medium saucepan, combine 1⅓ cups sugar, cornstarch and salt. Gradually stir in water; blend until smooth. Cook over medium heat until mixture boils, stirring constantly. Remove from heat. Stir about ½ cup hot mixture into egg yolks; add egg mixture to saucepan. Cook until mixture is bubbly. (Mixture will be very thick.) Remove from heat; stir in 2 tablespoons margarine, lemon peel and lemon juice. Pour filling over crust.

3 In small bowl, beat egg whites and cream of tartar at medium speed until soft peaks form, about 1 minute. Add ½ cup sugar 1 tablespoon at a time, beating at high speed until stiff peaks form and sugar is dissolved. Spread meringue over hot filling.

4 Bake at 350°F. for 25 to 30 minutes or until meringue is golden brown. Cool 30 minutes. Refrigerate at least 1 hour before serving. Cut into squares. Store in refrigerator.

12 servings

NUTRITION INFORMATION PER SERVING:
SERVING SIZE: 1/12 of Recipe

Calories	440	Calories from Fat	140
		% DAILY VALUE	
Total Fat	16 g	25%	
Saturated	4 g	20%	
Cholesterol	90 mg	30%	
Sodium	420 mg	18%	
Total Carbohydrate	71 g	24%	
Dietary Fiber	1 g	4%	
Sugars	49 g		
Protein	4 g		
Vitamin A	10%	Vitamin C	4%
Calcium	2%	Iron	8%

DIETARY EXCHANGES: 1-1/2 Starch, 3 Fruit, 3 Fat
OR 4-1/2 Carbohydrate, 3 Fat

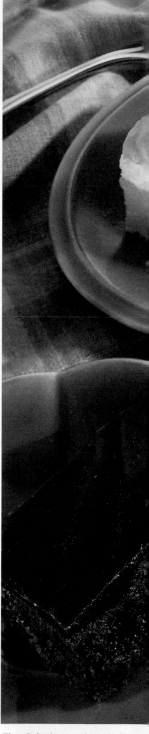

Tina Principato of West Roxbury, Massachusetts, created this springtime dessert for the 23rd BAKE-OFF® Contest.

Clockwise from top:
Lemon Meringue Dessert Squares,
Sour Cream Apple Squares p. 51,
Chocolate Cherry Bars p. 50

Eclectic Tastes of the '70s   49

Chocolate Cherry Bars

Pictured on page 48

Prep Time: 15 minutes (Ready in 2 hours)

Pictured on page 48

Recipe Fact

Frances Jerzak of Porter, Minnesota, won $25,000 for this quick and easy recipe.

Keep ingredients on hand for this yummy dessert. Requiring only 15 minutes of preparation time, it's perfect to make when you need an easy dessert.

Kitchen Tips

Prepare the frosting only after the bars have baked. If made ahead, the frosting will stiffen and become hard to spread.

An offset or angled metal spatula makes spreading frosting on bars quick and easy. The bent blade goes right to the sides and corners of the pan. Look for offset spatulas at kitchenware stores.

BARS
1 (1 lb. 2.25-oz.) pkg. Pillsbury Moist Supreme® Devil's Food Cake Mix
1 (21-oz.) can cherry pie filling
1 teaspoon almond extract
2 eggs, beaten

FROSTING
1 cup sugar
1/3 cup milk
5 tablespoons margarine or butter
1 (6-oz.) pkg. (1 cup) semi-sweet chocolate chips

1 Heat oven to 350°F. Grease and flour 15×10×1-inch baking pan or 13×9-inch pan. In large bowl, combine all bar ingredients; stir until well blended. Spread in greased and floured pan.

2 Bake at 350°F. until toothpick inserted in center comes out clean. For 15×10×1-inch pan, bake 20 to 30 minutes; for 13×9-inch pan, bake 25 to 30 minutes.

3 In small saucepan, combine sugar, milk and margarine; mix well. Bring to a boil. Boil 1 minute, stirring constantly. Remove from heat; stir in chocolate chips until smooth. Pour and spread over warm bars. Cool 1 1/4 hours or until completely cooled. Cut into bars.

48 bars

HIGH ALTITUDE (ABOVE 3500 FEET): For either size pan, bake at 375°F. for 25 to 30 minutes.

NUTRITION INFORMATION PER SERVING:
SERVING SIZE: 1 Bar

Calories	110	Calories from Fat	35
		% DAILY VALUE	
Total Fat	4 g	6%	
Saturated	1 g	5%	
Cholesterol	10 mg	3%	
Sodium	100 mg	4%	
Total Carbohydrate	18 g	6%	
Dietary Fiber	1 g	2%	
Sugars	14 g		
Protein	1 g		
Vitamin A	0%	Vitamin C	0%
Calcium	0%	Iron	4%

DIETARY EXCHANGES: 1/2 Starch, 1/2 Fruit, 1 Fat
OR 1 Carbohydrate, 1 Fat

Sour Cream Apple Squares

Pictured on page 49

Prep Time: 20 minutes (Ready in 1 hour 30 minutes)

2 cups Pillsbury BEST® All Purpose Flour
2 cups firmly packed brown sugar
½ cup margarine or butter, softened
1 cup chopped nuts
1 to 2 teaspoons cinnamon
1 teaspoon baking soda
½ teaspoon salt
1 (8-oz.) container sour cream
1 teaspoon vanilla
1 egg
2 cups finely chopped, peeled apples

1 Heat oven to 350°F. Lightly spoon flour into measuring cup; level off. In large bowl, combine flour, brown sugar and margarine; beat at low speed until crumbly. Stir in nuts. Press 2¾ cups crumb mixture in bottom of ungreased 13×9-inch pan.

2 To remaining mixture, add cinnamon, baking soda, salt, sour cream, vanilla and egg; mix well. Stir in apples. Spoon evenly over crumb mixture in pan.

3 Bake at 350°F. for 30 to 40 minutes or until toothpick inserted in center comes out clean. Cool 30 minutes. Cut into squares. Serve warm or cool; if desired, serve with whipped cream or ice cream. Store in refrigerator.

12 servings

HIGH ALTITUDE (ABOVE 3500 FEET):
Bake at 375°F. for 25 to 35 minutes.

NUTRITION INFORMATION PER SERVING:
SERVING SIZE: 1/12 of Recipe

Calories	410	Calories from Fat	160
		% DAILY VALUE	
Total Fat	18 g	28%	
Saturated	5 g	25%	
Cholesterol	25 mg	8%	
Sodium	310 mg	13%	
Total Carbohydrate	58 g	19%	
Dietary Fiber	2 g	8%	
Sugars	40 g		
Protein	5 g		
Vitamin A	10%	Vitamin C	0%
Calcium	8%	Iron	10%

DIETARY EXCHANGES: 1-1/2 Starch, 2-1/2 Fruit, 3-1/2 Fat
OR 4 Carbohydrate, 3-1/2 Fat

COOK'S NOTES

Recipe Fact
Luella Maki of Ely, Minnesota, took home the Grand Prize in 1975 for this simple apple cake. Her recipe is one of Pillsbury's most requested ones.

Serving Suggestions
Top this warm homemade apple cake with a scoop of cinnamon ice cream.

Baking this cake in a 13×9-inch pan makes it easy to tote to family gatherings and picnics. Use pressurized whipped cream in a can to garnish each serving. Carry the whipped cream in a cooler and keep it chilled when not in use.

Crescent Caramel Swirl

Pictured on right

Prep Time: 20 minutes (Ready in 55 minutes)

½ **cup butter (do not use margarine)**
½ **cup chopped nuts**
¾ **cup firmly packed brown sugar**
1 **tablespoon water**
2 **(8-oz.) cans Pillsbury Refrigerated Crescent Dinner Rolls**

1 Heat oven to 350°F. Melt butter in small saucepan. Coat bottom and sides of 12-cup Bundt® pan with 2 tablespoons of the melted butter; sprinkle pan with 3 tablespoons of the nuts. Add remaining nuts, brown sugar and water to remaining melted butter. Bring to a boil, stirring occasionally. Boil 1 minute, stirring constantly.

2 Remove dough from cans; do not unroll. Cut each long roll into 8 slices. Arrange 8 slices, cut side down, in nut-lined pan; separate layers of each pinwheel slightly. Spoon half of brown sugar mixture over dough. Place remaining 8 dough slices alternately over bottom layer. Spoon remaining brown sugar mixture over slices.

3 Bake at 350°F. for 23 to 33 minutes or until deep golden brown. Cool 3 minutes. Invert onto serving platter or waxed paper. Serve warm.

12 servings

NUTRITION INFORMATION PER SERVING:
SERVING SIZE: 1/12 of Recipe

Calories	290	Calories from Fat	160
		% DAILY VALUE	
Total Fat	18 g	28%	
Saturated	7 g	35%	
Cholesterol	20 mg	7%	
Sodium	370 mg	15%	
Total Carbohydrate	29 g	10%	
Dietary Fiber	1 g	3%	
Sugars	16 g		
Protein	3 g		
Vitamin A	6%	Vitamin C	0%
Calcium	2%	Iron	6%

DIETARY EXCHANGES: 1 Starch, 1 Fruit, 3-1/2 Fat
OR 2 Carbohydrate, 3-1/2 Fat

The judges at the 27th contest awarded Lois Ann Groves of San Antonio, Texas, $25,000 for her creative version of a pastry-shop caramel roll, Crescent Caramel Swirl.

From top:
Crescent Caramel Swirl,
Simply Super Crescent
Cinnamon Rolls p. 56

Whole Wheat Raisin Loaf

Pictured on right

Prep Time: 30 minutes (Ready in 4 hours)

Recipe Fact
Lenora Smith of Harahan, Louisiana, created this hearty whole wheat bread and became the Grand Prize Winner of the 27th BAKE-OFF® Contest in 1976.

Ingredient Info
Whole wheat flour is milled from the entire wheat kernel, including the germ. Because wheat germ contains fat, whole wheat flour is susceptible to spoilage. Store whole wheat flour in an airtight container in the refrigerator or freezer.

Baked products made with whole wheat flour have a heavier, more compact texture than those made with all purpose flour.

Storage Tip
Store raisins in a tightly closed container in a cool place, and they will last up to a year.

2 to 3 cups Pillsbury BEST® All Purpose Flour
½ cup sugar
3 teaspoons salt
1 teaspoon cinnamon
½ teaspoon nutmeg
2 pkg. active dry yeast
2 cups milk
¾ cup water
¼ cup oil
4 cups Pillsbury BEST® Whole Wheat Flour
1 cup rolled oats
1 cup raisins
1 tablespoon margarine or butter, melted
1 teaspoon sugar, if desired

1 Lightly spoon flour into measuring cup; level off. In large bowl, combine 1½ cups all purpose flour, ½ cup sugar, salt, cinnamon, nutmeg and yeast; mix well. In medium saucepan, heat milk, water and oil until very warm (120 to 130°F.). Add warm liquid to flour mixture; blend at low speed until moistened. Beat 3 minutes at medium speed. By hand, stir in whole wheat flour, rolled oats, raisins and an additional ¼ to ¾ cup all purpose flour until dough pulls cleanly away from sides of bowl.

2 On floured surface, knead in remaining ¼ to ¾ cup all purpose flour until dough is smooth and elastic, about 5 minutes. Place dough in greased bowl; cover loosely with greased plastic wrap and cloth towel. Let rise in warm place (80 to 85°F.) until light and doubled in size, 20 to 30 minutes.

3 Grease two 9×5 or 8×4-inch loaf pans. Punch down dough several times to remove all air bubbles. Divide dough in half; shape into loaves. Place in greased pans. Cover; let rise in warm place until light and doubled in size, 30 to 45 minutes.

4 Heat oven to 375°F. Uncover dough. Bake 40 to 50 minutes or until loaves are deep golden brown and sound hollow when lightly tapped. If loaves become too brown, cover loosely with foil during last 10 minutes of baking. Immediately remove from pans; cool on wire racks for 1½ hours or until completely cooled. Brush tops of loaves with margarine; sprinkle with 1 teaspoon sugar.

2 (16-slice) loaves

HIGH ALTITUDE (ABOVE 3500 FEET): No change.

NUTRITION INFORMATION PER SERVING:
SERVING SIZE: 1 Slice

Calories	160	Calories from Fat	25
		% DAILY VALUE	
Total Fat	3 g	5%	
Saturated	1 g	5%	
Cholesterol	0 mg	0%	
Sodium	210 mg	9%	
Total Carbohydrate	29 g	10%	
Dietary Fiber	3 g	12%	
Sugars	7 g		
Protein	5 g		
Vitamin A	0%	Vitamin C	0%
Calcium	4%	Iron	8%

Low-Fat

DIETARY EXCHANGES: 2 Starch **OR** 2 Carbohydrate

Simply Super
Crescent Cinnamon Rolls

Pictured on page 53

Prep Time: 15 minutes (Ready in 40 minutes)

Recipe Fact
This coiled cinnamon roll was created by Dorothy Veasey of Fort Wayne, Indiana, for the 24th BAKE-OFF® Contest. Her recipe is an easy alternative to preparing cinnamon rolls with homemade dough.

Make-Ahead Tip
Prepare and shape the rolls and place them in a greased 13×9-inch pan. Cover them with plastic wrap and refrigerate up to 2 hours. Bake as directed in the recipe, adding several additional minutes of baking time, if necessary.

Make It Special
For an indulgent treat, try drizzling the baked rolls with chocolate glaze.

ROLLS
- ⅔ cup finely chopped pecans
- ⅓ cup firmly packed brown sugar
- ⅓ cup powdered sugar
- 1 teaspoon cinnamon
- ¼ cup butter, softened
- 2 (8-oz.) cans Pillsbury Refrigerated Crescent Dinner Rolls

GLAZE
- 1 cup powdered sugar
- 1 tablespoon butter, softened
- 1 to 2 tablespoons milk

1 Heat oven to 375°F. Grease 13×9-inch pan. In small bowl, combine all roll ingredients except crescent rolls; mix well.

2 Unroll 1 can dough into 2 long rectangles. Overlap long sides to form 13×7-inch rectangle; firmly press perforations and edges to seal. Spread with nut mixture. Unroll second can of dough and shape into 13×7-inch rectangle as directed above. Place second rectangle over nut filling.

3 Cut into eight 13-inch strips. Twist each strip 5 or 6 times. Form each strip into a coil. Place in greased pan.

4 Bake at 375°F. for 20 to 25 minutes or until golden brown. Immediately remove from pan.

5 In small bowl, blend all glaze ingredients, adding enough milk for desired drizzling consistency. Drizzle over warm rolls. Serve warm.

8 large rolls

NUTRITION INFORMATION PER SERVING:
SERVING SIZE: 1 Large Roll

Calories	460	Calories from Fat	230
		% DAILY VALUE	
Total Fat	25 g	38%	
Saturated	8 g	40%	
Cholesterol	20 mg	7%	
Sodium	510 mg	21%	
Total Carbohydrate	54 g	18%	
Dietary Fiber	2 g	8%	
Sugars	32 g		
Protein	5 g		
Vitamin A	6%	Vitamin C	0%
Calcium	4%	Iron	10%

DIETARY EXCHANGES: 2 Starch, 1-1/2 Fruit, 4-1/2 Fat
OR 3-1/2 Carbohydrate, 4-1/2 Fat

Pecan Pie Surprise Bars

Pictured above

Prep Time: 15 minutes (Ready in 2 hours 40 minutes)

BASE
- 1 (1 lb. 2.25-oz.) pkg. Pillsbury Moist Supreme® Yellow or Butter Flavor Yellow Cake Mix
- ⅓ cup margarine or butter, softened
- 1 egg

FILLING
- ½ cup firmly packed brown sugar
- 1½ cups dark corn syrup
- 1 teaspoon vanilla
- 3 eggs
- 1 cup chopped pecans

1 Heat oven to 350°F. Grease 13×9-inch pan.
Reserve ⅔ cup of the dry cake mix for filling. In large
bowl, combine remaining dry cake mix, margarine
and 1 egg; beat at low speed until well blended.
Press in bottom of greased pan. Bake at 350°F.
for 15 to 20 minutes or until light golden brown.

continued on p. 58

Pecan Pie Surprise Bars — continued from p. 57

Ingredient Info

For the best flavor, always use pure vanilla extract. In our test kitchens, all recipes calling for vanilla are prepared with pure vanilla extract. Imitation vanilla contains artificial flavorings and can leave a bitter after-taste.

2 Meanwhile, in large bowl, combine reserved ²/₃ cup dry cake mix, brown sugar, corn syrup, vanilla and 3 eggs; beat at low speed until moistened. Beat 1 minute at medium speed or until well blended.

3 Remove pan from oven; pour filling mixture over warm base. Sprinkle with pecans. Return to oven; bake an additional 30 to 35 minutes or until filling is set. Cool 1½ hours or until completely cooled. Cut into bars. Store in refrigerator.

36 bars

HIGH ALTITUDE (ABOVE 3500 FEET): Add ⅓ cup flour to cake mix before removing ²/₃ cup for filling. Decrease corn syrup to 1¼ cups. Bake base at 375°F. for 15 to 20 minutes; bake filling at 375°F. for 30 to 35 minutes.

NUTRITION INFORMATION PER SERVING:

SERVING SIZE:	1 Bar			
Calories		160	Calories from Fat	50
			% DAILY VALUE	
Total Fat	6	g	9%	
Saturated	1	g	5%	
Cholesterol	25	mg	8%	
Sodium	140	mg	6%	
Total Carbohydrate	26	g	9%	
Dietary Fiber	1	g	2%	
Sugars	13	g		
Protein	1	g		
Vitamin A	2%		Vitamin C	0%
Calcium	0%		Iron	4%

DIETARY EXCHANGES: 1/2 Starch, 1 Fruit, 1-1/2 Fat **OR** 1-1/2 Carbohydrate, 1-1/2 Fat

COOK'S NOTES

Recipe Fact

At the 23rd BAKE-OFF® Contest, Mary Wilson of Leesburg, Georgia, was presented with a check for $5,000 for these rocky road bars. Her rich chocolate bars have since become a Pillsbury classic.

Rocky Road Fudge Bars

Pictured on page 47

Prep Time: 25 minutes (Ready in 2 hours 10 minutes)

BASE
½ cup margarine or butter
1 oz. unsweetened chocolate, cut up
1 cup Pillsbury BEST® All Purpose Flour
1 cup sugar
1 teaspoon baking powder
1 teaspoon vanilla
2 eggs
¾ cup chopped nuts

FILLING
1 (8-oz.) pkg. cream cheese, softened,
    reserving 2 oz. for frosting
¼ cup margarine or butter, softened
½ cup sugar
2 tablespoons Pillsbury BEST® All Purpose Flour
½ teaspoon vanilla
1 egg
¼ cup chopped nuts
1 (6-oz.) pkg. (1 cup) semi-sweet chocolate chips
2 cups miniature marshmallows

FROSTING
¼ cup margarine or butter
¼ cup milk
1 oz. unsweetened chocolate, cut up
   Reserved cream cheese
3 cups powdered sugar
1 teaspoon vanilla

1 Heat oven to 350°F. Grease and flour 13×9-inch pan. In large saucepan, melt ½ cup margarine and 1 oz. unsweetened chocolate over low heat, stirring until smooth. Remove from heat. Lightly spoon flour into measuring cup; level off. Stir in 1 cup flour and all remaining base ingredients; mix well. Spread in greased and floured pan.

2 In small bowl, combine 6 oz. of the cream cheese, ¼ cup margarine, ½ cup sugar, 2 tablespoons flour, ½ teaspoon vanilla and 1 egg; beat 1 minute at medium speed until smooth and fluffy. Stir in ¼ cup nuts. Spread over chocolate mixture; sprinkle evenly with chocolate chips.

3 Bake at 350°F. for 25 to 35 minutes or until toothpick inserted in center comes out clean. Remove from oven; immediately sprinkle with marshmallows. Return to oven; bake an additional 2 minutes.

4 While marshmallows are baking, in large saucepan, combine ¼ cup margarine, milk, 1 oz. unsweetened chocolate and reserved 2 oz. cream cheese. Cook over low heat, stirring until well blended. Remove from heat; stir in powdered sugar and 1 teaspoon vanilla until smooth. Immediately pour frosting over puffed marshmallows and lightly swirl with knife to marble. Refrigerate 1 hour or until firm. Cut into bars. Store in refrigerator.

Yield: 48 bars

HIGH ALTITUDE (ABOVE 3500 FEET): No change.

Kitchen Tips

To quickly soften cream cheese, remove it from the foil wrapper; microwave it on MEDIUM for 30 to 40 seconds.

To cut bars easily, begin by lining the pan with foil. Be sure to extend foil over the sides of the pan so you'll have enough to lift the bars out. Grease and flour the foil, then prepare and bake the bars as directed. Cool and refrigerate the baked bars for about 1 hour. Lift the bars from the pan. Remove the foil and cut into bars.

Storage Tip

Store these bars in a single layer in an airtight container in the refrigerator. For longer storage, freeze them in an airtight container for up to 3 months.

NUTRITION INFORMATION PER SERVING:
SERVING SIZE: 1 Bar

Calories	170	Calories from Fat	80
		% DAILY VALUE	
Total Fat	9 g	14%	
Saturated	3 g	15%	
Cholesterol	20 mg	7%	
Sodium	75 mg	3%	
Total Carbohydrate	21 g	7%	
Dietary Fiber	1 g	2%	
Sugars	17 g		
Protein	2 g		
Vitamin A	6%	Vitamin C	0%
Calcium	0%	Iron	2%

DIETARY EXCHANGES: 1 Starch, 1/2 Fruit, 1-1/2 Fat
OR 1-1/2 Carbohydrate, 1-1/2 Fat

The Adventurous '80s

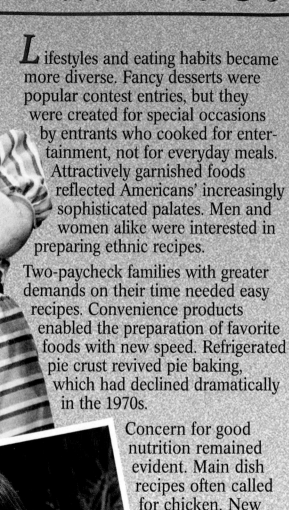

*L*ifestyles and eating habits became more diverse. Fancy desserts were popular contest entries, but they were created for special occasions by entrants who cooked for entertainment, not for everyday meals. Attractively garnished foods reflected Americans' increasingly sophisticated palates. Men and women alike were interested in preparing ethnic recipes.

Two-paycheck families with greater demands on their time needed easy recipes. Convenience products enabled the preparation of favorite foods with new speed. Refrigerated pie crust revived pie baking, which had declined dramatically in the 1970s.

Concern for good nutrition remained evident. Main dish recipes often called for chicken. New low-fat versions of dairy products were substituted for their traditional counterparts.

1. **Mary Lou Warren**, Colorado Springs, Colo., won top honors for her updated version of apple pie.

2. **Julie Konecne**, Bemidji, Minn., has lots of reasons to love her exquisite creation, Chocolate Praline Layer Cake, not the least of which earned her the top prize at the 33rd competition.

3. With microwave ovens becoming wildly popular during the 80s, microwave cooking editors were eager to meet and talk with finalists who used the new appliance so expertly.

4. Each BAKE-OFF® Contest commences with the Grand March, lead by celebrities such as George Pillsbury and Miss America, Susan Akin.

5. **Leonard Thompson** garnished his pie with the precision that you'd expect from this retired engineer.

Italian Zucchini Crescent Pie

Pictured on right

Prep Time: 30 minutes (Ready in 55 minutes)

Recipe Fact
Millicent Caplan of
Tamarac, Florida, brought
this creative main dish
to the 29th contest.
She was awarded top
honors for her recipe.

Kitchen Tip
To make this pie in a
12×8-inch (2-quart)
baking dish, unroll the
dough into 2 long rectan-
gles. Press the dough over
bottom and one inch up
sides of pan to form crust.
Firmly press perforations
to seal. Continue with
recipe as directed.

Serving Suggestion
Cutting the pie into
small wedges or squares
transforms this recipe
into a party appetizer.

2 tablespoons margarine or butter
4 cups thinly sliced zucchini
1 cup chopped onions
2 tablespoons dried parsley flakes
1/2 teaspoon salt
1/2 teaspoon pepper
1/4 teaspoon garlic powder
1/4 teaspoon dried basil leaves
1/4 teaspoon dried oregano leaves
2 eggs, well beaten
8 oz. (2 cups) shredded Muenster or
   mozzarella cheese
1 (8-oz.) can Pillsbury Refrigerated Crescent
   Dinner Rolls
2 teaspoons prepared mustard

1 Heat oven to 375°F. Melt margarine in 12-inch skillet over medium-high heat. Add zucchini and onions; cook and stir 6 to 8 minutes or until tender. Stir in parsley flakes, salt, pepper, garlic powder, basil and oregano.

2 In large bowl, combine eggs and cheese; mix well. Stir in cooked vegetable mixture.

3 Separate dough into 8 triangles. Place in ungreased 10-inch pie pan or 11-inch quiche pan; press over bottom and up sides to form crust. Firmly press perforations to seal. Spread crust with mustard. Pour egg mixture evenly into crust-lined pan.

4 Bake at 375°F. for 18 to 22 minutes or until knife inserted near center comes out clean. Cover edge of crust with strips of foil during last 10 minutes of baking if necessary to prevent excessive browning. Let stand 10 minutes before serving.

6 servings

NUTRITION INFORMATION PER SERVING:
SERVING SIZE: 1/6 of Recipe

Calories	370	Calories from Fat	230
		% DAILY VALUE	
Total Fat	25 g	38%	
Saturated	10 g	50%	
Cholesterol	105 mg	35%	
Sodium	790 mg	33%	
Total Carbohydrate	21 g	7%	
Dietary Fiber	2 g	8%	
Sugars	7 g		
Protein	15 g		
Vitamin A	20%	Vitamin C	10%
Calcium	30%	Iron	10%

DIETARY EXCHANGES: 1 Starch, 1 Vegetable,
1-1/2 High-Fat Meat, 2-1/2 Fat **OR** 1 Carbohydrate,
1 Vegetable, 1-1/2 High-Fat Meat, 2-1/2 Fat

Salted Peanut Chews

Pictured on right

Prep Time: 35 minutes (Ready in 1 hour 35 minutes)

Recipe Fact

Gertrude M. Schweitzerhof of Cupertino, California, brought this candy-like bar to the 29th contest held in Miami, Florida.

Ingredient Info

Tightly wrap leftover marshmallows and store them in the freezer. Frozen marshmallows will stay fresh and soft; just thaw at room temperature before using them.

Ingredient Substitution

Any salted nuts can be used in place of the peanuts.

Kitchen Tip

For easier cutting, dip the knife into hot water occasionally to eliminate the stickiness caused by the marshmallow layer.

CRUST

1½ cups Pillsbury BEST® All Purpose Flour
⅔ cup firmly packed brown sugar
½ teaspoon baking powder
½ teaspoon salt
¼ teaspoon baking soda
½ cup margarine or butter, softened
1 teaspoon vanilla
2 egg yolks
3 cups miniature marshmallows

TOPPING

⅔ cup corn syrup
¼ cup margarine or butter
2 teaspoons vanilla
1 (10-oz.) pkg. peanut butter chips
2 cups crisp rice cereal
2 cups salted peanuts

1 Heat oven to 350°F. Lightly spoon flour into measuring cup; level off. In large bowl, combine all crust ingredients except marshmallows at low speed until crumbly. Press firmly in bottom of ungreased 13×9-inch pan.

2 Bake at 350°F. for 12 to 15 minutes or until light golden brown. Remove from oven; immediately sprinkle with marshmallows. Return to oven; bake an additional 1 to 2 minutes or until marshmallows just begin to puff. Cool while preparing topping.

3 In large saucepan, combine all topping ingredients except cereal and peanuts. Heat just until chips are melted and mixture is smooth, stirring constantly. Remove from heat; stir in cereal and peanuts. Immediately spoon warm topping over marshmallows; spread to cover. Refrigerate 45 minutes or until firm. Cut into bars.

36 bars

HIGH ALTITUDE (ABOVE 3500 FEET): No change.

NUTRITION INFORMATION PER SERVING:
SERVING SIZE: 1 Bar

Calories	200	Calories from Fat	90
		% DAILY VALUE	
Total Fat	10 g	15%	
Saturated	2 g	10%	
Cholesterol	10 mg	3%	
Sodium	170 mg	7%	
Total Carbohydrate	23 g	8%	
Dietary Fiber	2 g	8%	
Sugars	13 g		
Protein	4 g		
Vitamin A	4%	Vitamin C	0%
Calcium	2%	Iron	4%

DIETARY EXCHANGES: 1 Starch, 1/2 Fruit, 2 Fat
OR 1-1/2 Carbohydrate, 2 Fat

Sachertorte Cookies

Pictured above

Prep Time: 1 hour 35 minutes

Recipe Fact

Sachertorte is the very rich cake created in 1832 by Franz Sacher. His Viennese family was famous for their hotels and restaurants. The classic recipe consists of three layers of chocolate cake filled with apricot jam. The cake is covered in chocolate glaze, and served with whipped cream. This simple cookie version of Sachertorte earned Phyllis Wolf of Salem, Oregon, $2,000 at the 30th contest.

1 cup margarine or butter, softened
1 (3.9-oz.) pkg. instant chocolate pudding and pie filling mix
1 egg
2 cups Pillsbury BEST® All Purpose Flour
3 tablespoons sugar
⅔ cup apricot or cherry preserves
½ cup semi-sweet chocolate chips
3 tablespoons margarine or butter

1 Heat oven to 325°F. In large bowl, combine 1 cup margarine and pudding mix; beat until light and fluffy. Add egg; blend well.

2 Lightly spoon flour into measuring cup; level off. Gradually add flour; mix well. Shape dough into 1-inch balls; roll in sugar. Place 2 inches apart on ungreased cookie sheets. With thumb, make indentation in center of each cookie.

3 Bake at 325°F. for 15 to 18 minutes or until firm to the touch. Immediately remove from cookie sheets. Cool 15 minutes or until completely cooled. Fill each indentation with ½ teaspoon preserves.

4 In small saucepan, melt chocolate chips and 3 tablespoons margarine over low heat, stirring until smooth. Drizzle glaze evenly over cookies.

4 dozen cookies

HIGH ALTITUDE (ABOVE 3500 FEET):
Bake at 350°F. for 12 to 15 minutes.

NUTRITION INFORMATION PER SERVING:

SERVING SIZE:	1 Cookie		
Calories	90	Calories from Fat	45
		% DAILY VALUE	
Total Fat	5 g	8%	
Saturated	1 g	5%	
Cholesterol	4 mg	1%	
Sodium	90 mg	4%	
Total Carbohydrate	11 g	4%	
Dietary Fiber	0 g	0%	
Sugars	6 g		
Protein	1 g		
Vitamin A	4%	Vitamin C	0%
Calcium	0%	Iron	2%

DIETARY EXCHANGES: 1/2 Starch, 1 Fat
OR 1/2 Carbohydrate, 1 Fat

Kitchen Tip

To reduce cleanup, place the chocolate chips and margarine in a small resealable plastic food storage bag. Microwave on MEDIUM until the chocolate and margarine are melted, about 2 to 3 minutes. Snip a tiny opening in one corner of the bag and drizzle the chocolate over the cooled cookies.

Storage Tip

After the chocolate glaze has set, pack cookies between layers of waxed paper in a covered container.

Chocolate Praline Layer Cake

Pictured on right

Prep Time: 25 minutes (Ready in 2 hours 15 minutes)

Recipe Fact
In 1988, Julie Konecne of Bemidji, Minnesota, was awarded the top prize for this outstanding chocolate cake. Her recipe is a favorite in the Pillsbury test kitchens.

Kitchen Tips
To make small chocolate curls, place a square of semi-sweet chocolate or a thick milk chocolate bar on a piece of foil. Let stand in a warm place (80 to 85°F.) until slightly softened, about 5 to 10 minutes. Using long strokes with a vegetable peeler, shave chocolate from bottom of the square or bar. Let curls drop to foil. Use a toothpick to transfer curls to the cake.

To make large chocolate curls, melt 4 ounces of semi-sweet chocolate. Use a rubber scraper to spread melted chocolate in a thin layer on two inverted cookie sheets. Refrigerate until chocolate is just firm but not brittle, about 10 minutes. Use a metal spatula or pancake turner to scrape chocolate from the pan, making curls. The width of the spatula will determine the width of the curls. Use a toothpick to transfer curls to the cake.

CAKE
½ **cup butter**
¼ **cup whipping cream**
1 **cup firmly packed brown sugar**
¾ **cup coarsely chopped pecans**
1 **(1 lb. 2.25-oz.) pkg. Pillsbury Moist Supreme®**
  Devil's Food Cake Mix
1¼ **cups water**
⅓ **cup oil**
3 **eggs**
TOPPING
1¾ **cups whipping cream**
¼ **cup powdered sugar**
¼ **teaspoon vanilla**
16 **whole pecans, if desired**
16 **chocolate curls, if desired**

1 Heat oven to 325°F. In small heavy saucepan, combine butter, ¼ cup whipping cream and brown sugar. Cook over low heat just until butter is melted, stirring occasionally. Pour into two 9 or 8-inch round cake pans; sprinkle evenly with chopped pecans.

2 In large bowl, combine cake mix, water, oil and eggs; beat at low speed until moistened. Beat 2 minutes at medium speed. Carefully spoon batter over pecan mixture.

3 Bake at 325°F. for 35 to 45 minutes or until cake springs back when touched lightly in center. Cool 5 minutes; remove from pans. Cool 1 hour or until completely cooled.

4 In small bowl, beat 1¾ cups whipping cream until soft peaks form. Add powdered sugar and vanilla; beat until stiff peaks form.

5 To assemble cake, place 1 layer on serving plate, praline side up. Spread with half of whipped cream. Top with second layer, praline side up; spread top with remaining whipped cream. Garnish with whole pecans and chocolate curls. Store in refrigerator.
16 servings

HIGH ALTITUDE (ABOVE 3500 FEET):
Add ⅓ cup flour to dry cake mix; increase water to 1⅓ cups. Bake at 350°F. for 30 to 35 minutes. Immediately remove from pans.

NUTRITION INFORMATION PER SERVING:
SERVING SIZE: 1/16 of Recipe

Calories	460	Calories from Fat	270
		% DAILY VALUE	
Total Fat	30 g	46%	
Saturated	13 g	65%	
Cholesterol	95 mg	32%	
Sodium	330 mg	14%	
Total Carbohydrate	43 g	14%	
Dietary Fiber	2 g	8%	
Sugars	30 g		
Protein	4 g		
Vitamin A	15%	Vitamin C	0%
Calcium	6%	Iron	10%

DIETARY EXCHANGES: 1-1/2 Starch, 1-1/2 Fruit, 5-1/2 Fat
OR 3 Carbohydrate, 5-1/2 Fat

Lemon Platinum Cake

Pictured on page 72

Prep Time: 55 minutes (Ready in 3 hours 10 minutes)

Pictured on page 72

Recipe Fact

Elizabeth Penney of San Diego, California, created this special-occasion dessert for the 33rd contest.

Kitchen Tips

When grating lemon peel, rub only the yellow part against the small holes of a grater. Or use a vegetable peeler or lemon zester to remove strips of peel. Finely chop the peel strips. One medium lemon yields approximately one table-spoon of grated peel.

To split the cake layers evenly, space toothpicks around the sides to form a cutting guide. Cut the cake with a long serrated knife. To prevent the layers from shifting, gently hold the top of the cake with one hand while slicing with the other.

CAKE
8 egg whites
1 teaspoon cream of tartar
½ teaspoon salt
1 cup sugar
7 egg yolks
1 cup Pillsbury BEST® All Purpose Flour
⅓ cup lemon juice
2 teaspoons grated lemon peel

FILLING
1 cup sugar
¼ cup cornstarch
Dash salt
1¼ cups water
2 egg yolks
3 tablespoons lemon juice
1 tablespoon margarine or butter
2 teaspoons grated lemon peel

TOPPING
2 cups whipping cream
3 to 4 drops yellow food color, if desired
2 kiwi fruit, peeled, sliced, if desired

1 Heat oven to 325°F. In large bowl, beat egg whites until foamy. Add cream of tartar and ½ teaspoon salt; beat until soft peaks form. Gradually add ½ cup of the sugar, beating until stiff peaks form. Set aside.

2 In small bowl, beat 7 egg yolks until lemon colored, about 2 minutes. Gradually add remaining ½ cup sugar, beating until thick and light lemon colored.

3 Lightly spoon flour into measuring cup; level off. Add flour, ⅓ cup lemon juice and 2 teaspoons lemon peel to egg yolk mixture; beat at low speed for 1 minute. By hand, gently fold egg yolk mixture into egg white mixture. Pour batter into ungreased 10-inch tube pan.

4 Bake at 325°F. for 40 to 55 minutes or until top springs back when touched lightly in center. Immediately invert cake onto funnel or narrow-necked glass bottle. Cool 1¼ hours or until completely cooled. Remove from pan.

5 While cake is cooling, in small saucepan, combine 1 cup sugar, cornstarch and dash salt; mix well. Gradually stir in water. Cook over medium heat until mixture boils and thickens, stirring constantly; remove from heat. In small bowl, beat 2 egg yolks; gradually blend small amount of hot mixture into egg yolks. Add egg yolk mixture to saucepan; cook over low heat for 2 to 3 minutes or until thickened, stirring constantly. Remove from heat; stir in all remaining filling ingredients. Cool 1 hour. Reserve ½ cup filling for topping.

6 In small bowl, beat whipping cream until slightly thickened. Add reserved ½ cup filling and food color; beat until thickened, about 30 seconds. DO NOT OVERBEAT.

7 To assemble cake, slice cake horizontally to make 3 layers. Place bottom layer on serving plate; spread with half (about ½ cup) of filling. Place middle layer on top; spread with remaining filling. Top with third layer. Spread sides, center and top of cake with topping. Refrigerate at least 1 hour before serving.

8 Just before serving, cut kiwi fruit slices in half; arrange on cake or garnish as desired. Store in refrigerator.

16 servings

HIGH ALTITUDE (ABOVE 3500 FEET): No change.

Make-Ahead Tip

The cooled, baked cake can be placed in a tightly sealed plastic cake container and frozen for up to 3 months. Thaw it at room temperature for 2 to 3 hours and fill, top and garnish as directed.

Make It Special

Garnish the platter and/or individual serving plates with lemon peel and mint leaves.

Serving Suggestion

With its fresh lemon filling and beautiful kiwi fruit garnish, this cake is a perfect choice for spring-time birthdays, showers or anniversaries.

NUTRITION INFORMATION PER SERVING:
SERVING SIZE: 1/16 of Recipe

Calories	300	Calories from Fat	140
		% DAILY VALUE	
Total Fat	15 g	23%	
Saturated	8 g	40%	
Cholesterol	165 mg	55%	
Sodium	130 mg	5%	
Total Carbohydrate	36 g	12%	
Dietary Fiber	1 g	3%	
Sugars	27 g		
Protein	5 g		
Vitamin A	15%	Vitamin C	15%
Calcium	4%	Iron	4%

DIETARY EXCHANGES: 1 Starch, 1-1/2 Fruit, 3 Fat
OR 2-1/2 Carbohydrate, 3 Fat

French Walnut Torte

Pictured on left

Prep Time: 35 minutes (Ready in 3 hours 20 minutes)

CAKE
1½ cups sugar
1 tablespoon vanilla
3 eggs
1¾ cups Pillsbury BEST® All Purpose Flour
2 teaspoons baking powder
½ teaspoon salt
1 cup ground walnuts
1½ cups whipping cream, whipped

GLAZE
½ cup apricot or peach preserves
1 tablespoon sugar

FROSTING
2 cups powdered sugar
½ cup margarine or butter, softened
½ teaspoon vanilla
1 (3-oz.) pkg. cream cheese, softened
½ cup ground walnuts

1 Heat oven to 350°F. Grease and flour two 9-inch round cake pans. In large bowl, combine 1½ cups sugar, 1 tablespoon vanilla and eggs; beat 5 minutes at high speed.

2 Lightly spoon flour into measuring cup; level off. In medium bowl, combine flour, baking powder and salt; mix well. Stir in 1 cup ground walnuts. Add flour mixture and whipped cream alternately to sugar mixture, beginning and ending with flour mixture; mix well. Pour into greased and floured pans.

3 Bake at 350°F. for 25 to 30 minutes or until cake springs back when touched lightly in center. Cool 15 minutes; remove from pans.

4 In small saucepan, combine glaze ingredients; heat until warm and sugar dissolves, stirring occasionally. Reserve ¼ cup glaze. Spread remaining glaze over top of warm layers. Refrigerate glazed layers and reserved glaze for 30 minutes.

continued on p. 74

This delicious from-scratch cake is truly worth the time it takes to make. Maureen Theroux of Ellenton, Florida, earned $2,000 for this recipe at the 29th BAKE-OFF® Contest.

From top: French Walnut Torte, Lemon Platinum Cake p. 70

French Walnut Torte — continued from p. 73

COOK'S NOTES

Kitchen Tips

Grind the walnuts in a food processor, a spice mill, or in batches in a blender. Use short on/off bursts to grind the nuts evenly, stirring them once or twice if necessary. Be careful to process the nuts only until they are finely ground, not pasty.

If the apricot pieces in the preserves are large, cut them into smaller pieces before heating the preserves and sugar.

Make It Special

Impress guests with this layered torte. Present the cake on a pedestal plate. If you don't have a pedestal plate, create one by placing a decorative glass plate on an overturned small glass dish.

5 In medium bowl, combine all frosting ingredients except ½ cup ground walnuts; beat 2 minutes at medium speed.

6 To assemble cake, place 1 layer on serving plate, glazed side up. Spread with half of frosting. Top with second layer, glazed side up; spread top with remaining frosting. Sprinkle with ½ cup ground walnuts. Refrigerate 30 minutes.

7 Spread reserved ¼ cup glaze on sides of cake. If desired, press an additional ½ cup ground walnuts into glaze. Refrigerate at least 1 hour before serving. Store in refrigerator.

16 servings

HIGH ALTITUDE (ABOVE 3500 FEET): Decrease sugar in cake to 1⅓ cups; decrease baking powder to 1¾ teaspoons. Bake at 375°F. for 25 to 30 minutes.

NUTRITION INFORMATION PER SERVING:
SERVING SIZE: 1/16 of Recipe

Calories	450	Calories from Fat	220
		% DAILY VALUE	
Total Fat	24 g		37%
Saturated	8 g		40%
Cholesterol	75 mg		25%
Sodium	240 mg		10%
Total Carbohydrate	54 g		18%
Dietary Fiber	1 g		4%
Sugars	40 g		
Protein	5 g		
Vitamin A	15%	Vitamin C	0%
Calcium	8%	Iron	6%

DIETARY EXCHANGES: 2 Starch, 1-1/2 Fruit, 4-1/2 Fat
OR 3-1/2 Carbohydrate, 4-1/2 Fat

Praline Crescent Dessert

Pictured on page 77

Prep Time: 30 minutes (Ready in 1 hour)

⅓ cup margarine or butter
½ cup firmly packed brown sugar
3 tablespoons sour cream
1 cup crisp rice cereal
½ cup chopped pecans or nuts
½ cup coconut
1 (8-oz.) can Pillsbury Refrigerated Crescent
    Dinner Rolls
1 (3-oz.) pkg. cream cheese, softened
2 tablespoons powdered sugar
    Whipping cream, whipped, if desired

1 Heat oven to 375°F. Melt margarine in medium saucepan over low heat. Add brown sugar; cook 2 minutes, stirring constantly. Add sour cream; cook 4 minutes, stirring occasionally. Remove from heat. Add cereal, pecans and coconut; stir until evenly coated.

2 Separate dough into 8 triangles. Place each triangle in ungreased muffin cup; press dough to cover bottom and sides.

3 In small bowl, combine cream cheese and powdered sugar; blend well. Spoon rounded teaspoonful into each cup; spread over bottom. Divide brown sugar mixture evenly into cups.

4 Bake at 375°F. for 11 to 16 minutes or until deep golden brown. Serve warm or cool, topped with whipped cream. Store in refrigerator.

8 servings

NUTRITION INFORMATION PER SERVING:
SERVING SIZE: 1/8 of Recipe

Calories	400	Calories from Fat	240
		% DAILY VALUE	
Total Fat	27 g	42%	
Saturated	9 g	45%	
Cholesterol	20 mg	7%	
Sodium	400 mg	17%	
Total Carbohydrate	34 g	11%	
Dietary Fiber	1 g	4%	
Sugars	20 g		
Protein	4 g		
Vitamin A	15%	Vitamin C	2%
Calcium	4%	Iron	8%

DIETARY EXCHANGES: 1-1/2 Starch, 1 Fruit, 5 Fat
OR 2-1/2 Carbohydrate, 5 Fat

COOK'S NOTES

Recipe Fact

At the 30th BAKE-OFF® Contest, Marjorie Hooper of Lakeland, Florida, won $15,000 for this simple dessert.

Ingredient Info

Packaged coconut is available in cans or plastic bags and in shredded or flaked form. Either form can be used in this recipe.

Make-Ahead Tip

Assemble the recipe; cover and refrigerate it for up to 2 hours. Bake as directed.

Serving Suggestion

The caramel-roll flavors of this dessert would also be perfect for a special brunch or breakfast treat.

Apple Nut Lattice Tart

Pictured on right

Prep Time: 30 minutes (Ready in 3 hours 25 minutes)

Recipe Fact

Mary Lou Warren of Colorado Springs, Colorado, took home the Grand Prize in 1986 for this elegant apple tart.

Ingredient Info

With all the types of apples available, it's hard to know which ones work well for baking. In our test kitchens, we have the greatest success with Braeburn and Gala apples. These two varieties bake up tender and moist and hold their shape during baking.

Golden raisins have been treated to prevent darkening as they dry. While dark raisins are sun-dried, golden raisins are dried with artificial heat, which produces a moister, plumper raisin. For recipes, dark and golden raisins are interchangeable.

CRUST
    1 (15-oz.) pkg. Pillsbury Refrigerated Pie Crusts
FILLING
    3 to 3½ cups (3 to 4 medium) thinly sliced, peeled apples
    ½ cup sugar
    3 tablespoons golden raisins
    3 tablespoons chopped walnuts or pecans
    ½ teaspoon cinnamon
    ¼ to ½ teaspoon grated lemon peel
    2 teaspoons lemon juice
GLAZE
    ¼ cup powdered sugar
    1 to 2 teaspoons lemon juice

1 Prepare pie crusts as directed on package for *two-crust pie* using 10-inch tart pan with removable bottom or 9-inch pie pan. Place 1 prepared crust in pan; press in bottom and up sides of pan. Trim edges if necessary.

2 Place cookie sheet in oven to preheat. Heat oven to 400°F. In large bowl, combine all filling ingredients; toss lightly to coat. Spoon into crust-lined pan.

3 To make lattice top, cut second crust into ½-inch-wide strips. Arrange strips in lattice design over filling. Trim and seal edges.

4 Place tart on preheated cookie sheet. Bake at 400°F. for 40 to 55 minutes or until apples are tender and crust is golden brown. Cover edge of crust with strips of foil during last 10 to 15 minutes of baking if necessary to prevent excessive browning. Remove from cookie sheet. Cool 1 hour.

5 In small bowl, blend glaze ingredients, adding enough lemon juice for desired drizzling consistency. Drizzle over slightly warm tart. Cool 1 hour or until completely cooled. Remove sides of pan.

8 servings

NUTRITION INFORMATION PER SERVING:
SERVING SIZE: 1/8 of Recipe

Calories	360	Calories from Fat	140
		% DAILY VALUE	
Total Fat	16 g	25%	
Saturated	6 g	30%	
Cholesterol	15 mg	5%	
Sodium	210 mg	9%	
Total Carbohydrate	53 g	18%	
Dietary Fiber	2 g	8%	
Sugars	26 g		
Protein	2 g		
Vitamin A	0%	Vitamin C	4%
Calcium	0%	Iron	4%

DIETARY EXCHANGES: 1 Starch, 2-1/2 Fruit, 3 Fat
OR 3-1/2 Carbohydrate, 3 Fat

From top: Apple Nut Lattice Tart, Praline Crescent Dessert p. 75

Recipe Fact
At the 33rd BAKE-OFF®
Contest, Stephanie
Luetkehans of Chicago,
Illinois, won $2,000
for these rich and
flavorful muffins.

Kitchen Tip
Quick breads like these
muffins become tough
if the batter is overmixed.
For tender muffins,
combine the ingredients
with a fork or spoon just
until the dry ingredients
are moistened.

Make It Special
For sparkly, sugar-crusted
muffins, sprinkle the batter
with sugar after filling the
muffin cups.

*From top: Country Apple
Coffee Cake p.81, Lemon
Raspberry Muffins,
Raspberry Ripple
Crescent Coffee
Cake p. 80*

Lemon Raspberry Muffins
Pictured below

Prep Time: 15 minutes (Ready in 45 minutes)

2 cups Pillsbury BEST® All Purpose Flour
1 cup sugar
3 teaspoons baking powder
½ teaspoon salt
1 cup half-and-half
½ cup oil
1 teaspoon lemon extract
2 eggs
1 cup fresh or frozen raspberries
   without syrup (do not thaw)

1 Heat oven to 425°F. Line 12 muffin cups
with paper baking cups. Lightly spoon flour into
measuring cup; level off. In large bowl, combine
flour, sugar, baking powder and salt; mix well.

2 In small bowl, combine half-and-half, oil,
lemon extract and eggs; blend well. Add to dry
ingredients; stir just until dry ingredients are
moistened. Carefully fold in raspberries. Divide
batter evenly into paper-lined muffin cups.

3 Bake at 425°F. for 18 to 23 minutes or until
golden brown. Cool 5 minutes; remove from pans.
12 muffins

HIGH ALTITUDE (ABOVE 3500 FEET): Line 16 muffin
cups with paper baking cups. Decrease baking powder
to 2 teaspoons. Bake as directed above. **16 muffins**

NUTRITION INFORMATION PER SERVING:

SERVING SIZE:	1 Muffin			
Calories	260		Calories from Fat	110
		% DAILY VALUE		
Total Fat	12 g	18%		
Saturated	3 g	15%		
Cholesterol	45 mg	15%		
Sodium	230 mg	10%		
Total Carbohydrate	35 g	12%		
Dietary Fiber	1 g	4%		
Sugars	19 g			
Protein	4 g			
Vitamin A	4%	Vitamin C		4%
Calcium	10%	Iron		8%

DIETARY EXCHANGES: 1-1/2 Starch, 1 Fruit, 2 Fat
OR 2-1/2 Carbohydrate, 2 Fat

Raspberry Ripple Crescent Coffee Cake

Pictured on page 79

Prep Time: 20 minutes (Ready in 1 hour)

Recipe Fact

The flavors of an Austrian linzertorte inspired Priscilla Yee of Concord, California, to create this yummy custard-like coffee cake.

Kitchen Tips

Grated lemon peel is very aromatic and recipes often call for small amounts of it. To keep grated lemon peel on hand, grate the entire lemon, wrap the peel tightly in plastic wrap and freeze it. Frozen lemon peel takes only a few minutes to thaw at room temperature.

The type of baking pan you choose affects baking times. If your baking pan has a dark finish, the coffee cake will probably be done in the minimum baking time. Conversely, if you have an insulated pan, the baking time will probably be the longest time in the range.

COFFEE CAKE
3/4 **cup sugar**
1/4 **cup margarine or butter, softened**
2 **eggs**
3/4 **cup ground almonds**
1/4 **cup Pillsbury BEST® All Purpose Flour**
1 **teaspoon grated lemon peel**
1 **(8-oz.) can Pillsbury Refrigerated Crescent Dinner Rolls**
8 **teaspoons raspberry preserves**
1/4 **cup sliced almonds**

GLAZE
1/3 **cup powdered sugar**
1 **to 2 teaspoons milk**

1 Heat oven to 375°F. Grease 9-inch round cake pan or 9-inch pie pan. In large bowl, combine sugar, margarine and eggs; beat until smooth. Add ground almonds, flour and lemon peel; mix well. Set aside.

2 Separate dough into 8 triangles. Spread 1 teaspoon preserves on each triangle. Roll up, starting at shortest side of triangle and rolling to opposite point. Place rolls in greased pan in 2 circles, arranging 5 rolls around outside edge and 3 in center. Pour and carefully spread almond mixture evenly over rolls. Sprinkle with almonds.

3 Bake at 375°F. for 27 to 37 minutes or until coffee cake is deep golden brown and center is set. If necessary, cover coffee cake with foil during last 5 to 10 minutes of baking to prevent excessive browning.

4 In small bowl, blend glaze ingredients, adding enough milk for desired drizzling consistency. Drizzle over warm cake. Serve warm.

8 servings

NUTRITION INFORMATION PER SERVING:
SERVING SIZE: 1/8 of Recipe

Calories	380	Calories from Fat	170
		% DAILY VALUE	
Total Fat	19 g	29%	
Saturated	3 g	15%	
Cholesterol	55 mg	18%	
Sodium	300 mg	13%	
Total Carbohydrate	45 g	15%	
Dietary Fiber	2 g	8%	
Sugars	29 g		
Protein	6 g		
Vitamin A	6%	Vitamin C	0%
Calcium	4%	Iron	8%

DIETARY EXCHANGES: 2 Starch, 1 Fruit, 3-1/2 Fat
OR 3 Carbohydrate, 3-1/2 Fat

Country Apple Coffee Cake

Pictured on page 79

Prep Time: 20 minutes (Ready in 1 hour 10 minutes)

COFFEE CAKE
- 2 tablespoons margarine or butter, softened
- 1½ cups chopped peeled apples
- 1 (12-oz.) can Hungry Jack® Refrigerated Flaky Biscuits
- ⅓ cup firmly packed brown sugar
- ¼ teaspoon cinnamon
- ⅓ cup light corn syrup
- 1½ teaspoons whiskey, if desired
- 1 egg
- ½ cup pecan halves or pieces

GLAZE
- ⅓ cup powdered sugar
- ¼ teaspoon vanilla
- 1 to 2 teaspoons milk

1 Heat oven to 350°F. Using 1 tablespoon of the margarine, generously grease 9-inch round cake pan or 8-inch square pan. Spread 1 cup of the apples in greased pan.

2 Separate dough into 10 biscuits; cut each into quarters. Arrange biscuit pieces, points up, over apples. Top with remaining ½ cup apples.

3 In small bowl, combine remaining 1 tablespoon margarine, brown sugar, cinnamon, corn syrup, whiskey and egg; beat 2 to 3 minutes or until sugar is partially dissolved. Stir in pecans. Spoon over biscuit pieces and apples.

4 Bake at 350°F. for 35 to 45 minutes or until deep golden brown. Cool 5 minutes. If desired, remove from pan.

5 In small bowl, blend all glaze ingredients, adding enough milk for desired drizzling consistency. Drizzle over warm cake. Serve warm or cool. Store in refrigerator.

8 servings

NUTRITION INFORMATION PER SERVING:
SERVING SIZE: 1/8 of Recipe

Calories	330	Calories from Fat	130
		% DAILY VALUE	
Total Fat	14 g	22%	
Saturated	2 g	10%	
Cholesterol	25 mg	8%	
Sodium	510 mg	21%	
Total Carbohydrate	47 g	16%	
Dietary Fiber	2 g	8%	
Sugars	24 g		
Protein	4 g		
Vitamin A	4%	Vitamin C	0%
Calcium	2%	Iron	8%

DIETARY EXCHANGES: 1-1/2 Starch, 1-1/2 Fruit, 2-1/2 Fat **OR** 3 Carbohydrate, 2-1/2 Fat

COOK'S NOTES

Recipe Fact
Susan Porubcan of Whitewater, Wisconsin, created a biscuit coffee cake that combines pastry-shop appearance with down-home flavors. She won the Grand Prize at the 31st contest held in 1984.

Ingredient Info
Brown sugar is white sugar flavored and colored with molasses. Dark brown sugar has more molasses and therefore a more intense flavor than light brown sugar. Either type of brown sugar can be used in this recipe.

Storage Tip
Refrigerate shelled pecans in an airtight container for up to 3 months or freeze them for up to 6 months.

Cooking "American" in the '90s

*T*oday, ethnic cooking concepts are being fused to create a new "melting pot" cuisine. Tastes have become more international and people crave ethnic flavors. Formerly "gourmet" ingredients have gone mainstream.

Men are making their mark at the BAKE-OFF® Contest. The greatest number of men – 14 – competed at the 38th contest. Perhaps even more significant, the first BAKE-OFF® finalist to win the $1 million Grand Prize was a man.

Entries reflect trends toward convenience. New recipe categories focus on easy preparation and include a broader array of Pillsbury products to encourage solutions to everyday cooking challenges.

1. Choosing one favorite is nearly impossible as onlookers are dazzled by the display of all 100 winning recipes at the 35th BAKE-OFF® Contest.

2. A television crew captures Denver finalist Birdie Casement as she takes a break from the competition to share cooking tips.

3. And the winner is... Gladys Fulton from Summerville, S.C.

4. BAKE-OFF® hosts, George and Sally Pillsbury, greet guests with help from the Green Giant Sprout and Pillsbury Doughboy.

5. Finalists concentrate to cook or bake a winner.

Chicken Fajita Pizza

Pictured above

Prep Time: 20 minutes (Ready in 40 minutes)

Recipe Fact

Fajitas are a popular food of the '90s. Elizabeth Daniels of Kula, Maui, Hawaii, created this delicious fajita pizza for the 34th contest.

1 (10-oz.) can Pillsbury Refrigerated
    All Ready Pizza Crust
1 tablespoon olive or vegetable oil
4 boneless skinless chicken breast halves,
    cut into thin strips
1 to 2 teaspoons chili powder
½ to 1 teaspoon salt
½ teaspoon garlic powder
1 cup thinly sliced onions
1 cup green or red bell pepper strips (2×¼-inch)
½ cup Old El Paso® Salsa
8 oz. (2 cups) shredded Monterey Jack cheese

1 Heat oven to 425°F. Grease 12-inch pizza pan or 13×9-inch pan. Unroll dough; place in greased pan. Starting at center, press out with hands. Bake at 425°F. for 7 to 9 minutes or until very light golden brown.

From left: Chicken Fajita Pizza, Tuscany Pasta Toss p. 86

2 Meanwhile, heat oil in large skillet over medium-high heat until hot. Add chicken; sprinkle with chili powder, salt and garlic powder. Cook and stir 3 to 5 minutes or until lightly browned. Add onions and bell pepper strips; cook and stir an additional 2 to 3 minutes or until chicken is no longer pink and vegetables are crisp-tender.

3 Remove crust from oven. Spoon chicken mixture evenly over partially baked crust. Spoon salsa over chicken; sprinkle with cheese. Return to oven; bake an additional 14 to 18 minutes or until crust is golden brown.

8 servings

NUTRITION INFORMATION PER SERVING:
SERVING SIZE: 1/8 of Recipe

Calories	290	Calories from Fat	120
		% DAILY VALUE	
Total Fat	13 g	20%	
Saturated	6 g	30%	
Cholesterol	60 mg	20%	
Sodium	810 mg	34%	
Total Carbohydrate	20 g	7%	
Dietary Fiber	1 g	4%	
Sugars	3 g		
Protein	24 g		
Vitamin A	15%	Vitamin C	15%
Calcium	20%	Iron	10%

DIETARY EXCHANGES: 1-1/2 Starch, 2-1/2 Very Lean Meat, 2 Fat **OR** 1-1/2 Carbohydrate, 2-1/2 Very Lean Meat, 2 Fat

Make-Ahead Tip

This pizza goes together quickly for a delicious weeknight meal. To save time, prep the ingredients early in the day. Cut the chicken into strips, or purchase precut chicken strips. Cut the bell peppers and slice the onions. Shred the cheese or purchase shredded cheese. Wrap the ingredients separately and refrigerate them until it's time to assemble the pizza.

Make It Special

For a colorful pizza, use a combination of green, red and yellow bell pepper strips.

Tuscany Pasta Toss

Pictured on page 85

Prep Time: 20 minutes

Pictured on page 85

Recipe Fact

In 1998, the first Quick & Easy BAKE-OFF® Contest was held in Orlando, Florida. Recipes had to be fast, and the number of ingredients was kept to a minimum in one category. This 20-minute main dish recipe created by Susan Burns of Trenton, New Jersey, is delicious!

Ingredient Substitution

Six ounces of dry fettuccine, prepared according to package directions, can be substituted for the refrigerated fettuccine.

Serving Suggestion

Serve this meatless main dish with *Cheese-Crusted Flat Bread p. 40.* Finish the meal with one of our classic BAKE-OFF® cookies, such as *Split Seconds p. 11.*

1 (9-oz.) pkg. refrigerated fettuccine
2 cups chopped tomatoes
⅓ cup chopped fresh basil
1 (4.5-oz.) jar Green Giant® Sliced Mushrooms, drained
3 tablespoons olive or vegetable oil
2 tablespoons balsamic vinegar
1 tablespoon minced garlic in water (from 4.5-oz. jar)
½ teaspoon salt
¼ teaspoon cracked black pepper
4 oz. Gorgonzola or blue cheese, crumbled (1 cup)
½ cup chopped walnuts
Fresh basil leaves, if desired

1 Cook fettuccine to desired doneness as directed on package. Drain.

2 Meanwhile, in large serving bowl, combine tomatoes, chopped basil, mushrooms, oil, vinegar, garlic, salt and pepper; mix well.

3 Add cooked fettuccine; toss to coat. Add cheese and walnuts; mix gently. Garnish with basil leaves.

4 (1½-cup) servings

NUTRITION INFORMATION PER SERVING:
SERVING SIZE: 1-1/2 Cups

Calories	530	Calories from Fat	280
		% DAILY VALUE	
Total Fat	31 g	48%	
Saturated	8 g	40%	
Cholesterol	85 mg	28%	
Sodium	790 mg	33%	
Total Carbohydrate	45 g	15%	
Dietary Fiber	4 g	16%	
Sugars	4 g		
Protein	18 g		
Vitamin A	20%	Vitamin C	25%
Calcium	20%	Iron	20%

DIETARY EXCHANGES: 3 Starch, 1 High-Fat Meat, 4 Fat
OR 3 Carbohydrate, 1 High-Fat Meat, 4 Fat

Funfetti Cookies

Pictured above

Prep Time: 40 minutes

**1 (1 lb. 2.9-oz.) pkg. Pillsbury Moist Supreme®
Funfetti® Cake Mix**
⅓ cup oil
2 eggs
**½ (15.6-oz.) can Pillsbury Creamy Supreme®
Funfetti® Pink Vanilla Frosting**

1 Heat oven to 375°F. In large bowl, combine cake mix, oil and eggs; stir by hand until thoroughly moistened. Shape dough into 1-inch balls; place 2 inches apart on ungreased cookie sheets. With bottom of glass dipped in flour, flatten to ¼-inch thickness.

2 Bake at 375°F. for 6 to 8 minutes or until edges are light golden brown. Cool 1 minute; remove from cookie sheets.

3 Spread frosting over warm cookies. Immediately sprinkle each cookie with candy bits from frosting. Let frosting set before storing. Store in tightly covered container.

3 dozen cookies

continued on p. 88

Recipe Fact
These festive cookies earned Molly Taylor of Maryville, Tennessee, $2,000 at the 34th contest.

Just For Kids
With only four ingredients and 40 minutes of time involved, this recipe is a great choice to use when teaching children how to bake.

Funfetti Cookies — continued from p. 87

Storage Tip
After the frosting has set, store the cookies between layers of waxed paper in a covered container. To freeze the cookies, place them on cookie sheets and freeze. Package the frozen cookies in a rigid container with layers of waxed paper between them.

HIGH ALTITUDE (ABOVE 3500 FEET): Add ½ cup flour to dry cake mix. Bake as directed above.

NUTRITION INFORMATION PER SERVING:

SERVING SIZE:	1 Cookie		
Calories	110	Calories from Fat	45
		% DAILY VALUE	
Total Fat	5 g	8%	
Saturated	1 g	5%	
Cholesterol	10 mg	3%	
Sodium	105 mg	4%	
Total Carbohydrate	16 g	5%	
Dietary Fiber	0 g	0%	
Sugars	11 g		
Protein	1 g		
Vitamin A	0%	Vitamin C	0%
Calcium	0%	Iron	2%

DIETARY EXCHANGES: 1/2 Starch, 1/2 Fruit, 1 Fat **OR** 1 Carbohydrate, 1 Fat

COOK'S NOTES

Recipe Fact
At the 34th contest, Jean Olson of Wallingford, Iowa, won $2,000 for this gooey, filled chocolate cookie.

Ingredient Info
Unsweetened cocoa is pure cocoa powder with no ingredients added. Do not substitute powdered drink mix for the cocoa in this recipe.

Caramel-Filled Chocolate Cookies

Pictured on right

Prep Time: 1 hour 15 minutes

2½ cups Pillsbury BEST® All Purpose Flour
¾ cup unsweetened cocoa
1 teaspoon baking soda
1 cup sugar
1 cup firmly packed brown sugar
1 cup margarine or butter, softened
2 teaspoons vanilla
2 eggs
1 cup chopped pecans
48 Rolo® Chewy Caramels in Milk Chocolate, unwrapped (from 13-oz. pkg.)
1 tablespoon sugar
4 oz. vanilla-flavored candy coating, if desired

1 Lightly spoon flour into measuring cup; level off. In medium bowl, combine flour, cocoa and baking soda; mix well.

2 In large bowl, combine 1 cup sugar, brown sugar and margarine; beat until light and fluffy. Add vanilla and eggs; beat well. Add flour mixture; blend well. Stir in ½ cup of the pecans. If necessary, cover with plastic wrap; refrigerate 30 minutes for easier handling.

3 Heat oven to 375°F. For each cookie, with floured hands, shape about 1 tablespoon dough around 1 caramel candy, covering completely.

4 In small bowl, combine remaining ½ cup pecans and 1 tablespoon sugar. Press one side of each ball into pecan mixture. Place, nut side up, 2 inches apart on ungreased cookie sheets.

5 Bake at 375°F. for 7 to 10 minutes or until set and slightly cracked. Cool 2 minutes; remove from cookie sheets. Cool on wire rack for 15 minutes or until completely cooled.

6 Melt candy coating in small saucepan over low heat, stirring constantly until smooth. Drizzle over cookies.

4 dozen cookies

HIGH ALTITUDE (ABOVE 3500 FEET): Increase flour to 2¾ cups. Bake as directed above.

NUTRITION INFORMATION PER SERVING:

SERVING SIZE:	1 Cookie		
Calories	160	Calories from Fat	70
		% DAILY VALUE	
Total Fat	8 g	12%	
Saturated	2 g	10%	
Cholesterol	10 mg	3%	
Sodium	85 mg	4%	
Total Carbohydrate	20 g	7%	
Dietary Fiber	1 g	4%	
Sugars	14 g		
Protein	2 g		
Vitamin A	4%	Vitamin C	0%
Calcium	2%	Iron	4%

DIETARY EXCHANGES: 1-1/2 Starch, 1 Fruit, 2 Fat
OR 2-1/2 Carbohydrate, 2 Fat

Kitchen Tip

To evenly drizzle the cookies with vanilla-flavored coating, place the melted coating in a small squeeze bottle. Or place the vanilla coating in a resealable plastic food storage bag and microwave on MEDIUM until melted, about 2 minutes. Knead the coating until completely melted and smooth, then push it to one bottom corner of the bag. Snip a tiny tip from the corner of the bag to form an opening for squeezing out the coating.

Tuxedo Brownie Torte

Pictured on page 93

Prep Time: 40 minutes (Ready in 4 hours 10 minutes)

At the 35th BAKE-OFF®
Contest, Patricia Lapiezo
of LaMesa, California,
prepared this spectacular
brownie dessert. It tastes
as fabulous as it looks!

Kitchen Tips

Decorating tips and parch-
ment, plastic or plastic-lined
decorating bags are available at kitchenware stores
and some large grocery
stores. To use a decorating
bag, place a large star tip
in the bottom of the bag.
Place the empty bag in a
large tumbler and fold half
the bag down over and all
around the rim of the glass,
exposing the inside of the
bag. Or hold the bag in
your hand and fold the
bag down over your hand.
Fill the bag half full with
topping. Fold up the top
half of the bag, then twist
or roll down the top of
the bag to the level of the
topping. With one hand,
squeeze from the top of the
bag, while guiding the tip
with the other hand.

BROWNIE
  1 (1 lb. 3.5-oz.) pkg. Pillsbury Rich & Moist
    Fudge Brownie Mix
  ½ cup water
  ½ cup oil
  1 egg
FILLING
  1 (10-oz.) pkg. frozen raspberries in syrup, thawed
  1 tablespoon sugar
  1 tablespoon cornstarch
  1 cup fresh raspberries or frozen whole
    raspberries without syrup, thawed, drained
    on paper towel, reserving 3 for garnish
TOPPING
  1 (8-oz.) pkg. cream cheese, softened
  ⅓ cup powdered sugar
  2 tablespoons white creme de cacao, if desired
  1 cup white vanilla chips, melted
  1 cup whipping cream, whipped
GARNISH
  1 tablespoon grated semi-sweet chocolate
  3 whole fresh or frozen raspberries, if desired
  3 mint leaves, if desired

1 Heat oven to 350°F. Grease bottom and sides of
9 or 10-inch springform pan. In large bowl, combine
all brownie ingredients. Beat 50 strokes with spoon.
Spread batter in greased pan.

2 Bake at 350°F. for 38 to 45 minutes or until
center is set. Cool 30 minutes. Run knife around
sides of pan to loosen; remove sides of pan. Cool
30 minutes or until completely cooled.

3 In blender container or food processor bowl
with metal blade, blend thawed raspberries with
syrup until smooth. Place strainer over small
bowl; pour berries into strainer. Press berries with
back of spoon through strainer to remove seeds;
discard seeds.

4 In small saucepan, combine sugar and cornstarch. Gradually add raspberry puree; mix well. Bring to a boil. Cook until mixture is clear, stirring constantly. Cool 5 minutes. Spread over brownie layer to within ½ inch of edges. Arrange 1 cup fresh raspberries evenly over raspberry mixture; refrigerate.

5 In medium bowl, combine cream cheese, powdered sugar and creme de cacao; beat until smooth. Add melted vanilla chips; beat until smooth. Fold in whipped cream. Cover; refrigerate 45 minutes.

6 Stir topping mixture until smooth. Spread 1½ cups of the topping over raspberries. Pipe or spoon on remaining topping as desired. Refrigerate at least 1 hour or until firm.

7 Before serving, sprinkle grated chocolate in 1-inch border around outside edge of torte. Garnish center with 3 whole raspberries and 3 mint leaves. Store in refrigerator.

16 servings

HIGH ALTITUDE (ABOVE 3500 FEET): Add ¼ cup flour to dry brownie mix. Bake as directed above.

NUTRITION INFORMATION PER SERVING:

SERVING SIZE:	1/16 of Recipe		
Calories	420	Calories from Fat	220
		% DAILY VALUE	
Total Fat	24 g	37%	
Saturated	10 g	50%	
Cholesterol	50 mg	17%	
Sodium	150 mg	6%	
Total Carbohydrate	46 g	15%	
Dietary Fiber	2 g	8%	
Sugars	36 g		
Protein	4 g		
Vitamin A	10%	Vitamin C	6%
Calcium	6%	Iron	6%

DIETARY EXCHANGES: 1 Starch, 2 Fruit, 5 Fat **OR** 3 Carbohydrate, 5 Fat

Kitchen Tips *(continued)*

For the smoothest topping, warm the cream cheese in the microwave so it is the same temperature as the melted vanilla chips.

Make It Special

Instead of garnishing the center of the dessert with fresh raspberries and mint leaves, cut the dessert into wedges and garnish each wedge.

Serving Suggestion

Serve slices of this torte with cups of strong raspberry- or chocolate-flavored coffee.

Fudge Crostata with Raspberry Sauce

Pictured on right

Prep Time: 50 minutes (Ready in 3 hours 10 minutes)

Recipe Fact
Entered in the special-occasion dessert category in 1990, this elegant tart won Paula Cassidy of Berkeley, California, $10,000.

Kitchen Tips
To save time making the raspberry sauce, don't strain the seeds from the raspberry puree. The sauce will still look and taste wonderful.

To make the best whipped cream, use a tall narrow bowl and thoroughly chill the cream, bowl and beaters by placing them in the freezer until they are well chilled. Pour cold whipping cream into the well-chilled bowl; beat until soft peaks form. Blend in the vanilla and sugar, continuing to beat just until stiff peaks form.

CRUST
1 (15-oz.) pkg. Pillsbury Refrigerated Pie Crusts
FILLING
1 (6-oz.) pkg. (1 cup) semi-sweet chocolate chips
1/2 cup butter
2/3 cup sugar
1 cup ground almonds
1 egg
1 egg yolk
SAUCE
1 (12-oz.) pkg. frozen raspberries without syrup, thawed
3/4 cup sugar
1 teaspoon lemon juice
Sweetened whipped cream, if desired
Chocolate curls, if desired
Whole raspberries, if desired

1 Prepare pie crusts as directed on package for *two-crust pie* using 10-inch tart pan with removable bottom or 9-inch pie pan. Place 1 prepared crust in pan; press in bottom and up sides of pan. Trim edges if necessary.

2 Place cookie sheet in oven to preheat. Heat oven to 375°F. In small saucepan, melt chocolate chips and 2 tablespoons of the butter over low heat, stirring constantly until smooth. In medium bowl, combine remaining 6 tablespoons butter and 2/3 cup sugar; beat until light and fluffy. Add almonds, 1 egg, egg yolk and melted chocolate; blend well. Spread mixture evenly over bottom of crust-lined pan.

3 To make lattice top, cut second crust into 1/2-inch-wide strips. Arrange strips in lattice design over chocolate mixture. Trim and seal edges.

4 Place tart on preheated cookie sheet. Bake at 375°F. for 45 to 50 minutes or until crust is golden brown. If necessary, cover edge of crust with strips of foil during last 10 to 15 minutes of baking to prevent excessive browning. Cool 1 1/2 hours or until completely cooled.

5 Meanwhile, in blender container or food processor bowl with metal blade, blend raspberries at high speed until smooth. Place strainer over small saucepan; pour berries into strainer. Press berries with back of spoon through strainer to remove seeds; discard seeds. Add 3/4 cup sugar and lemon juice; blend well. Bring mixture to a boil, stirring constantly. Reduce heat to medium-low; boil 3 minutes, stirring constantly. Cool; refrigerate until serving time.

continued on p. 94

From top:
Tuxedo Brownie
Torte p. 90,
Fudge Crostata
with Raspberry
Sauce

Fudge Crostata with Raspberry Sauce — continued from p. 92

Kitchen Tips *(continued)*

Whipping cream doubles in volume after it is whipped. To make 2 cups of whipped cream, begin with 1 cup of whipping cream. To sweeten the whipped cream, add ½ teaspoon of vanilla and 2 tablespoons of powdered sugar or superfine sugar.

For directions on making chocolate curls, see the Kitchen Tip on p. 68.

6 Before serving, garnish crostata with whipped cream, chocolate curls and whole raspberries. Serve with raspberry sauce. Store in refrigerator.

12 servings

NUTRITION INFORMATION PER SERVING:
SERVING SIZE: 1/12 of Recipe

Calories	500	Calories from Fat	250
		% DAILY VALUE	
Total Fat	28 g		43%
Saturated	13 g		65%
Cholesterol	70 mg		23%
Sodium	230 mg		10%
Total Carbohydrate	57 g		19%
Dietary Fiber	3 g		12%
Sugars	37 g		
Protein	4 g		
Vitamin A	10%	Vitamin C	10%
Calcium	6%	Iron	8%

DIETARY EXCHANGES: 1 Starch, 3 Fruit, 5-1/2 Fat
OR 4 Carbohydrate, 5-1/2 Fat

COOK'S NOTES

Recipe Fact

Elizabeth Zemelko of Knox, Indiana, created these dainty tarts to bring to the 34th BAKE-OFF® Contest. Her recipe is perfect for a springtime party tray.

Ingredient Substitution

One-half cup of apricot preserves mixed with ½ cup of drained crushed pineapple can be used in place of the pineapple preserves.

Hawaiian Cookie Tarts

Pictured on right

Prep Time: 35 minutes (Ready in 2 hours 40 minutes)

COOKIES
1¾ cups Pillsbury BEST® All Purpose Flour
½ cup powdered sugar
2 tablespoons cornstarch
1 cup margarine or butter, softened
1 teaspoon vanilla

FILLING
1 cup pineapple preserves
½ cup sugar
1 egg
1½ cups coconut
Powdered sugar

1 Heat oven to 350°F. Lightly spoon flour into measuring cup; level off. In large bowl, combine flour, ½ cup powdered sugar and cornstarch; mix well. Add margarine and vanilla; with spoon, stir until soft dough forms. Shape dough into 1-inch balls. Place 1 ball in each of 36 ungreased miniature muffin cups; press in bottom and up sides of each cup.

2 Spoon 1 teaspoon pineapple preserves into each dough-lined cup. In small bowl, combine sugar and egg; beat with fork until well blended. Add coconut; stir until well coated with egg mixture. Spoon 1 teaspoon coconut mixture over preserves in each cup.

3 Bake at 350°F. for 23 to 33 minutes or until cookie crusts are very light golden brown. Cool in pans 20 minutes.

4 To release cookies from cups, hold muffin pan upside down at an angle over wire rack. With handle of table knife, firmly tap bottom of each cup until cookie releases. Cool 15 minutes or until completely cooled. Just before serving, sprinkle with powdered sugar.

3 dozen cookie tarts

HIGH ALTITUDE (ABOVE 3500 FEET): No change.

NUTRITION INFORMATION PER SERVING:
SERVING SIZE: 1 Cookie Tart

Calories	130	Calories from Fat	50
		% DAILY VALUE	
Total Fat	6 g	9%	
Saturated	4 g	20%	
Cholesterol	20 mg	7%	
Sodium	65 mg	3%	
Total Carbohydrate	17 g	6%	
Dietary Fiber	0 g	0%	
Sugars	10 g		
Protein	1 g		
Vitamin A	4%	Vitamin C	0%
Calcium	0%	Iron	2%

DIETARY EXCHANGES: 1/2 Starch, 1/2 Fruit, 1-1/2 Fat **OR** 1 Carbohydrate, 1-1/2 Fat

Kitchen Tip

Use a fine-gauge mesh tea strainer to evenly dust these tarts with powdered sugar. Place the powdered sugar in the strainer and tap it over the tarts, or use a teaspoon to stir the powdered sugar in the strainer, causing a dusting of sugar to fall onto the tarts.

Lemon Truffle Pie

Pictured on right

Prep Time: 1 hour 10 minutes (Ready in 3 hours 10 minutes)

Recipe Fact
Patricia Kiewiet of
LaGrange, Illinois,
competed at the
34th contest with this
excellent creamy pie.

Kitchen Tips
To toast the almonds,
spread them on a cookie
sheet; bake at 350°F. for
5 to 7 minutes until light
golden brown, stirring
occasionally. Or spread
the almonds in a thin layer
in a microwave-safe pie
pan. Microwave on HIGH
for 4 to 7 minutes or
until light golden brown,
stirring frequently.

When stirring the hot
mixture into the egg yolks,
use a whisk and stir briskly
to prevent pieces of the
egg yolk from solidifying
before they get blended
into the mixture.

CRUST
  1 Pillsbury Refrigerated Pie Crust
    (from 15-oz. pkg.)
FILLING
  1 cup sugar
  2 tablespoons cornstarch
  2 tablespoons Pillsbury BEST® All Purpose Flour
  1 cup water
  2 egg yolks, beaten
  1 tablespoon margarine or butter
  ½ teaspoon grated lemon peel
  ¼ cup lemon juice
  6 oz. (1 cup) white vanilla chips or chopped
    white chocolate baking bar
  1 (8-oz.) pkg. ⅓-less-fat cream cheese
    (Neufchatel), softened
TOPPING
  ½ cup whipping cream
  1 tablespoon sliced almonds, toasted

1 Heat oven to 450°F. Prepare pie crust as directed on package for *one-crust baked shell* using 9-inch pie pan. Bake at 450°F. for 9 to 11 minutes or until light golden brown. Cool 30 minutes or until completely cooled.

2 Meanwhile, in medium saucepan, combine sugar, cornstarch and flour; mix well. Gradually stir in water until smooth. Cook over medium heat until mixture boils, stirring constantly. Reduce heat; cook 2 minutes, stirring constantly.

3 Remove from heat. Stir about ¼ cup of hot mixture into egg yolks; blend well. Add egg yolk mixture to mixture in saucepan. Cook over medium-low heat until mixture comes to a boil, stirring constantly. Cook 2 minutes, stirring constantly.

4 Remove from heat. Stir in margarine, lemon peel and lemon juice. Transfer ⅓ cup hot filling to small saucepan; cool remaining lemon mixture 15 minutes. Add vanilla chips to hot filling in saucepan; stir over low heat just until chips are melted.

5 In small bowl, beat cream cheese until fluffy. Add melted vanilla chip mixture; beat until well blended. Spread over bottom of cooled baked shell. Spoon lemon mixture over cream cheese layer. Refrigerate 2 to 3 hours or until set.

6 In another small bowl, beat whipping cream until stiff peaks form. Pipe or spoon over pie. Garnish with toasted almonds. Store in refrigerator.
10 servings

NUTRITION INFORMATION PER SERVING:
SERVING SIZE: 1/10 of Recipe

Calories	410	Calories from Fat	210
		% DAILY VALUE	
Total Fat	23 g	35%	
Saturated	12 g	60%	
Cholesterol	85 mg	28%	
Sodium	210 mg	9%	
Total Carbohydrate	45 g	15%	
Dietary Fiber	0 g	0%	
Sugars	32 g		
Protein	5 g		
Vitamin A	10%	Vitamin C	2%
Calcium	8%	Iron	2%

DIETARY EXCHANGES: 1-1/2 Starch, 1-1/2 Fruit, 4-1/2 Fat
OR 3 Carbohydrate, 4-1/2 Fat

Cranberry Cream Cheese Coffee Cake

Pictured on right

Prep Time: 20 minutes (Ready in 1 hour 30 minutes)

Recipe Fact
This delicious coffee cake was created by Jeffrey Robasse of Buffalo, Minnesota, for the 37th BAKE-OFF® Contest.

Ingredient Substitutions
Pillsbury Date Quick Bread Mix can be used in place of the Cranberry Quick Bread Mix.

Chopped pecans or almonds can be substituted for the walnuts.

Serving Suggestion
Enjoy the remaining cranberry sauce as a spread on a turkey sandwich.

COFFEE CAKE
1 (15.6-oz.) pkg. Pillsbury Cranberry Quick Bread Mix
½ cup milk
1 tablespoon butter, softened
1 egg

FILLING
½ cup canned jellied cranberry sauce
4 oz. cream cheese, softened
¼ cup sugar

TOPPING
½ cup coarsely chopped walnuts
¼ cup butter, softened

1. Heat oven to 350°F. Grease 9-inch square or 11×7-inch pan. Reserve 1 cup quick bread mix for topping. In medium bowl, combine remaining quick bread mix, milk, 1 tablespoon butter and egg; blend well. Spread batter in greased pan.

2. In food processor bowl with metal blade or blender container, combine all filling ingredients; process until smooth. Spread over batter in pan.

3. In small bowl, combine reserved 1 cup quick bread mix and walnuts; mix well. With pastry blender or fork, cut in ¼ cup butter until mixture resembles coarse crumbs. Sprinkle over filling.

4. Bake at 350°F. for 30 to 40 minutes or until light golden brown. Cool 30 minutes. Serve warm or cool. Store in refrigerator.

12 servings

HIGH ALTITUDE (ABOVE 3500 FEET): Add 1 tablespoon flour to dry quick bread mix before dividing. Bake as directed above.

NUTRITION INFORMATION PER SERVING:
SERVING SIZE: 1/12 of Recipe

Calories	290	Calories from Fat	120
		% DAILY VALUE	
Total Fat	13 g	20%	
Saturated	6 g	30%	
Cholesterol	40 mg	13%	
Sodium	240 mg	10%	
Total Carbohydrate	40 g	13%	
Dietary Fiber	1 g	4%	
Sugars	25 g		
Protein	4 g		
Vitamin A	8%	Vitamin C	0%
Calcium	4%	Iron	6%

DIETARY EXCHANGES: 1-1/2 Starch, 1 Fruit, 2-1/2 Fat
OR 2-1/2 Carbohydrate, 2-1/2 Fat

COOK'S NOTES

Recipe Fact

Reminiscent of an old-world specialty, this apple dumpling-in-custard casserole won Sharon Richardson of Dallas, Texas, $10,000 in the 34th BAKE-OFF® contest.

Ingredient Info

Amaretto is an almond-flavored liqueur but is often produced from the kernel of apricot pits rather than almonds.

Serving Suggestions

Try this casserole when you are entertaining for breakfast or brunch. Place the pie dish in a basket lined with a colorful napkin.

Since it's best served warm, coordinate your menu and oven use so this coffee cake can be served warm from the oven.

Country French Apple Crescent Casserole

Pictured on right

Prep Time: 25 minutes (Ready in 1 hour 5 minutes)

DUMPLINGS

2 tablespoons sugar
½ to 1 teaspoon cinnamon
1 (8-oz.) can Pillsbury Refrigerated Crescent Dinner Rolls
1 large apple, peeled, cut into 8 slices

SAUCE

½ cup sugar
½ cup whipping cream
1 tablespoon almond extract or amaretto
1 egg

TOPPING

½ cup sliced almonds
Cinnamon

1. Heat oven to 375°F. In small bowl, combine 2 tablespoons sugar and ½ to 1 teaspoon cinnamon; mix well. Separate dough into 8 triangles; sprinkle sugar mixture evenly over each. Gently press sugar mixture into each triangle, flattening each slightly.
2. Place apple slice on shortest side of each triangle; tuck in edges around apple slice. Roll up, starting at shortest side and rolling to opposite point. Seal all seams. Place point side down in ungreased 9-inch round baking dish or pie pan, placing long side of 7 filled crescents around outside edge of dish and 1 in center.
3. Bake at 375°F. for 15 to 20 minutes or until golden brown.
4. Remove baking dish from oven. In small bowl, combine all sauce ingredients; beat with wire whisk until well blended. Spoon sauce evenly over partially baked rolls. Sprinkle with almonds and cinnamon.
5. Return to oven; bake an additional 13 to 18 minutes or until deep golden brown. If necessary, cover with foil during last 5 minutes of baking to prevent excessive browning. Serve warm. Store in refrigerator.

8 servings

NUTRITION INFORMATION PER SERVING:
SERVING SIZE: 1/8 of Recipe

Calories	280	Calories from Fat	140
		% DAILY VALUE	
Total Fat	15 g	23%	
Saturated	5 g	25%	
Cholesterol	45 mg	15%	
Sodium	230 mg	10%	
Total Carbohydrate	32 g	11%	
Dietary Fiber	2 g	8%	
Sugars	21 g		
Protein	4 g		
Vitamin A	6%	Vitamin C	0%
Calcium	4%	Iron	6%

DIETARY EXCHANGES: 1 Starch, 1 Fruit, 3 Fat
OR 2 Carbohydrate, 3 Fat

index

French Silk Chocolate Pie p. 6

how to use our nutrition information

The key to healthy eating is a varied diet including many fruits, vegetables and grains. The detailed nutrition information in Classic® Cookbooks can help you estimate the contribution of specific recipes in your overall menu plan. At the end of each recipe, we list the calories per serving as well as the amount of fat, cholesterol, sodium, carbohydrate, dietary fiber, sugars, protein, vitamins A and C, calcium and iron.

- Each recipe also lists Percent Daily Values (% DVs). The % DVs tell you how much the nutrients in one serving of food contribute to a 2000-calorie diet. For example, if the DV for total fat is 10%, this means one serving of this food contributes 10% of the total fat suggested for a person on 2000 calories per day.

- We also include dietary exchanges for those of you who prefer this nutritional "accounting" method over traditional calorie watching. If you are following a medically prescribed diet, consult your physician or registered dietitian about this nutrition information.

How to Calculate Nutrition Information:

To determine a serving size for calculating nutrients for a recipe, we base our analysis on a single unit (for example, 1 cookie) or a specific amount (1 cup).

Other considerations for calculating nutrition information are:

- The first ingredient mentioned when the recipe gives options—for example, if "butter or margarine" is listed, butter would be calculated

- The larger amount of an ingredient when there's a range

- Garnishing or "if desired" ingredients when included in the ingredient list

- The estimated amount of marinade or frying oil absorbed during preparation

Tailoring Your Daily Diet

The chart below outlines some average daily nutritional needs for moderately active adults. Since your sex, age, size and activity level all affect dietary considerations, your requirements may deviate from those shown here.

What You Need Daily	Women Age: 25–50	Women Over 50	Men 25–50
Calories	2200	1900	2900
Total Fat	73 g or less	63	97
Saturated Fat	24 g or less	21	32
Cholesterol	300 mg or less	300	300
Sodium	2400 mg	2400	2400
Calcium	800 mg	800	800
Iron	15 mg	10	10

(Note: Although individual needs vary, a 2000-calorie diet is used as the reference diet on packaging because it approximates average daily requirements and provides a round number for easier calculating.)

Our Experts Behind the Scenes:

Our team of professionals, including registered dietitians and home economists, is dedicated to delivering comprehensive nutrition information to make your job of planning nutritious menus for you and your family just a little easier. Current information from the USDA and food manufacturer's labels are used to provide up-to-date nutrient values.

Swiss Ham Ring-Around p. 29

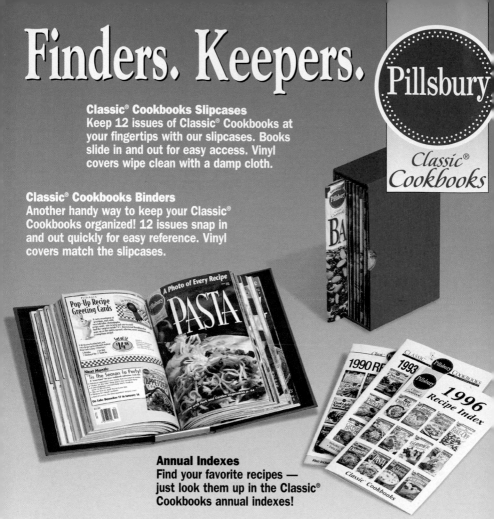